ELOQUENT LINE

CONTEMPORARY

JAPANESE

CALLIGRAPHY

ELOQUENT LINE

INTERNATIONAL

SCULPTURE

CENTER

1993

This catalogue was published on the occasion of an exhibition organized by the International Sculpture Center, Washington, D.C., the Sankei Shimbun and the Sankei International SHO Association, titled *Eloquent Line: Contemporary Japanese Calligraphy*. Support of the exhibition was provided by the Embassy of Japan, the Japan-United States Friendship Commission, Fujisankei Communications Group, Fujisankei Communications International, Inc ,with the cooperation of Japan Airlines.

Exhibition coordinated by Carla Hanzal, Thomas Yarker and David M. Furchgott

For information regarding the exhibition and catalogue, contact:

ISC Exhibition Services
1050 17th Street, N.W. Suite 250
Washington, D.C. 20036
tel: 202.785.1144
fax: 202.785.0810

ISBN 0-9633638-1-6
Catalogue designed by McEver Design, Washington, D.C. Catalogue printed by Expert/Brown, Richmond, Virginia
© 1992 International Sculpture Center, Washington, D.C.

Since 1986 the International Sculpture Center has been assisting art organizations in Japan in bringing exhibitions of Western art from North America and Europe to present to Japanese audiences. Now it is with equal pleasure that we are able to reciprocate by presenting to Americans the contemporary version of one of the most venerated Eastern art forms.

The artistic ties between Japan and the United States during the last century is under-explored terrain. There has been active exchange from both directions in the realms of architecture, graphic and fashion design, ceramics and a number of the craft-media related art forms. These trans-Pacific ties are often readily acknowledged. But, in the so-called "fine arts," — painting and sculpture, the mutual appropriation of artistic resources may not be as easily recognized. Nonetheless, between East and West there exists an exchange of linear idioms between calligraphy and painting.

We owe much thanks to our collaborators with the Sankei International SHO Association for their efforts toward the realization of this exchange. Special thanks to Kindo Hayashi, their President, for his patience in bridging two worlds. We also thank Kioshi Matsumoto, Eishi Itoh, Tadao Hiromi, Yukihide Yamashita and Akira Suzuki of the Sankei Shimbun for their steadfast coordination; and Masato Asai and Cheryl Silverman of the Fujisankei Communications Group for their vision and guidance. Toward the publication of this catalogue, we have received support from the Japan-U.S. Friendship Commission. We are also indebted to Samuel Hoi, Dean of the Corcoran School of Art, for arranging the premiere venue at the Corcoran Gallery of Art in Washington, D.C. ISC Exhibitions Director Carla Hanzal and Exhibitions Coordinator Tom Yarker have proven to be extraordinary navigators in guiding this bicultural vessel to safe harbor.

This exhibition allows us an opportunity to marvel in the complexity of simplicity, and to revel in the similarity of difference.

DAVID FURCHGOTT
EXECUTIVE
DIRECTOR
INTERNATIONAL
SCULPTURE CENTER

SHIGEAKI HAZAMA
PRESIDENT
THE SANKEI
SHIMBUN

The Sankei Shimbun is extremely pleased to have organized, with the International Sculpture Center and the Sankei International SHO Association, the "Eloquent Line: Contemporary Japanese Calligraphy" exhibition in the United States.

The Sankei International SHO Association was established in 1983, and is comprised of 750 participating members actively committed to the development of this traditional art in present-day Japan. The association holds a competitive annual exhibition which in 1993 drew over 10,000 entries. Fifty-eight of these have been selected for the exhibition at the Corcoran Gallery of Art's Hemicycle Gallery as representative of the best of contemporary Japanese calligraphy. We anticipate that the exhibition will offer a significant introduction of this art form to the American public. We hope it will also provide an opportunity to reflect on certain American art movements that have been influenced by Japanese calligraphy, and to contemplate the exchanges of different cultures that has taken place in the art world. Although it is an art based on the written word, we believe that SHO has the power to transcend language barriers and remind us of all that we share in common.

I hope that the exhibition will serve as a contribution to increased understanding between Japan and the United States, and would like to thank and extend my deepest respect and appreciation to the International Sculpture Center, the Corcoran Gallery of Art, the Embassy of Japan, Japan Airlines and all those responsible for making "Eloquent Line: Contemporary Japanese Calligraphy" possible.

産経新聞社
代表取締役社長　羽佐間重彰

ごあいさつ

　この度アメリカ合衆国ワシントンD.C.で、産経国際書会の代表作家による「線は語る―近代日本書道」と題する書展を開催する運びとなりました。産経国際書会は、産経新聞社が１９８３年に組織した、新しく活気溢れる書団体です。現在日本の伝統芸術である書道を伝承すべく約７５０人の指導者会員がその活動に情熱を傾けています。今年で１０回を数える日本の展覧会には、会員の門下生などから、約１万点の作品が出品される予定で、腕を競いあっています。

　この私たちの産経国際書会を代表する書家５８名による本展は、日本の現在の書芸術を、広くアメリカの方々に知っていただく大変良い機会と思われます。特に私たちは本展が、皆様アメリカの方々にとっては「東洋の異国文化」に触れる機会になったということに留まらず、米国芸術の形成にどのように日本の書が影響をもたらしたか、一方、私たち日本人にとっては、米国の抽象美術がいかに日本の書に影響を与えたか、日米双方の文化交流を理解していただけるよう企画いたしました。文字の表現にもかかわらず、まさしく言葉の壁を超えた芸術を通じ、お互いの文化や伝統的な価値観の違いを認め合い、より友好が深まるよう期待します。

　異国文化に感動する眼をもって、政治や経済の諸問題を超えた市民レベルでの心の通い合いが、両国間の恒久的な平和と協調関係を維持できることを祈り、本展の開催に御尽力いただいた国際彫刻センターをはじめコーコラン美術館、駐米日本大使館、日本航空ほか、関係各位に厚く御礼申し上げます。

The Sankei International SHO Association takes great pride in being able to present Japanese contemporary calligraphy at the Corcoran Gallery of Art in Washington, D.C. "Eloquent Line: Contemporary Japanese Calligraphy" marks our 10th exhibition abroad, and our first in the United States.

More than 15 million people in Japan practice the art of calligraphy. There are few, however, with a sense of the universal appeal of this art . We are deeply grateful to the International Sculpture Center and the Corcoran Gallery of Art for their vision and commitment to a comprehensive exhibition in the United States.

SHO is motion. Through the artist's dexterity, the flow of the lines expresses emotion appeals to the vision of the viewer. In this sense, SHO has also had an important influence on the Abstract Expressionist movement in Europe and the United States. I hope that presentation of this essentially Eastern form will stimulate renewed international interaction.

Daisetsu Suzuki, an international authority on Zen Buddhism, has said: "Whatever definition may be given to art, it is based on the experimentation of consciousness. 'Satori,' enlightenment, is the Zen term to describe the brief moment

when the pinnacle of creative inspiration is achieved. The artist experiences a heightened level of refinement and is spiritually moved." Development of technical skill is a basic prerequisite of grasping the spirit of SHO. Beyond this, the expression of the artist's character, inner dignity, wisdom and awareness rests on the accumulation of spiritual training and discipline.

We hope that those who view this exhibition will be touched by the Eastern thought reflected in the lines of SHO. At the same time, the opportunity to exhibit here will enrich the artists represented.

KINDŌ HAYASHI
CHAIRMAN
SANKEI INTERNATIONAL
SHO ASSOCIATION

産経国際書会が第10回展を迎え、これを記念してワシントンDCコーコラン美術館で「線は語る―近代日本書道」と題して、現代日本の書の諸相を紹介することとなりました。

日本では書道に興味を持ち制作や発表をする人々は1、500万人といわれます。然し、書の国際的な普遍性を意識して活動する作家や集団は極めて少なく、デモンストレーションやフェスティバルとして書を紹介するだけでは本当の書の国際的交流と発展にはなりません。

ISCはこの点に深い関心を持ち、産経新聞社と産経国際書会と共同で、コーコラン美術館としては初めての書展を開くことになりました。その先見性と熱意に深く敬意を表わします。

書は中国・日本で発達した文字を素材とし、作者の思考・人格・感動を表現し訴求するところの書線のモーションです。また書は文字の構成の条件を巧みに応用して造形性を視覚に訴えており、欧米の抽象絵画にも多くの影響を与えています。

このような書の東洋的思考を背景として、抽象美術との相互交流の中から、新たな国際的美術の創造を図るよう努力していきたいと思います。書の神韻を把握するということは書の技術を基本の条件として、書作する者自信の品格・教養・知性という、人間の内面的修練の積み重ねが、現代に生きている感覚として表現されるものであることを言います。

東洋的思考の反映として書線の造型を通して私達の訴えようとするものを味わって頂きたいと思います。私達もまたアメリカの近代的最先端の感性をとり入れて更に国際的な書芸術の創作に努力していきたいと思います。

産経国際書会
理事長 林 錦洞

THE ORIGINS AND EVOLUTION OF JAPANESE CALLIGRAPHY

BY CECIL H. UYEHARA

THE TRADITION OF JAPANESE CALLIGRAPHY. The Chinese system of writing using ideograms was introduced in Japan via Korea in the 5th or 6th century A.D. The Chinese script of the Later Han (1st to 3rd centuries), Northern Wei (3rd to 4th centuries) and Sui (6th to 7th centuries) dynasties came to Japan after some delay. It was the first of five waves of calligraphic influence to reach Japan from China. Each wave came to Japan many years after it had originated in China. A one-way relationship in calligraphy persisted until the Communists took over the Chinese government in 1949. For many years thereafter, because of the political situation there was essentially no relationship between China and Japan concerning calligraphy. In the meantime, Japanese calligraphers had an unusual and exhilarating interchange with Western abstract art in which the Chinese did not participate. For the past 20 years, however, there has been an exchange of calligraphers, artworks and exhibitions between Japan and China so energetic that it appears to be trying to make up for lost time. There now exists, for the first time in almost 1,500 years, a dialogue between calligraphers of China and Japan.

In China each ideogram or character has a given pronunciation that does not change in different grammatical contexts. The adaptation of this system to Japanese, a language with a completely different linguistic structure, was a laborious process. The imported Chinese characters were slowly transformed into two 50-character syllabaries (sets of written symbols) to accommodate the structure of the Japanese language. These syllabaries were a unique Japanese contribution to Oriental calligraphy.

Calligraphy was not only the method of communication for governance in ancient China and Japan, it also came to be accepted as the artistic equal of poetry and painting.[1] In the 7th and 8th centuries came the second wave from China, the brilliant calligraphic achievements of the Tang court (7th to 10th centuries) were brought to Japan and absorbed by the Nara and Heian aristocracies. The Heian era (8th to 12th centuries) showed the highest respect for the arts and calligraphy. An expert calligraphic hand was required for participation in the governmental and political processes, and it was expected for success in romantic relationships; indeed, the worth of one's personality was judged by one's calligraphic artistry. Although the value of calligraphy has been diluted in this modern age, a strong tradition still lingers. To this day, the Japanese regard and emulate Tang as one of the heights of the art of calligraphy.

Another wave brought Zen Buddhism into Japan from China during the 12th to 16th centuries. Zen's insistence on meditation, austerity and spiritual concentration appealed to Japan's dominant warrior class. Their calligraphies were vigorous, blunt, symbolic of strength; calligraphic line and vigor was regarded as a stern reflection of personality. For centuries there has been creative tension and competition between this so-called Zen-Chinese (karayo) style and the more sinuous, delicate, "romantic" Japanese style (wayo) of the Heian tradition. Differences in stylistic tradition, though difficult for the modern eye to detect, are still present in Japanese calligraphy.

The next wave came during the early 17th century, bringing the late

Ming (14th to 17th centuries) and early Manchu (17th to 20th centuries) calligraphic styles. This fourth wave coincided with the consolidation of military power by Tokugawa Ieyasu in 1603, who became Shogun and created the Shogunate system that lasted until 1868. In contrast to those of earlier eras, this Shogunate's administrative demands required writing ability. Calligraphy thus became accessible to and a necessity for many classes of people throughout the land: the imperial court, the military classes, merchants and particularly townspeople with administrative responsibilities. A wide variety of calligraphic styles, both Japanese and Chinese, developed and became available through the woodblock printing process. The foundation for modern Japanese calligraphy was built during this period of isolation, peace and rising prosperity.

The last wave came in 1881 when over 10,000 calligraphic items were brought to Japan by a member of the Imperial Chinese Embassy, and a long forgotten Chinese style of calligraphy of the Six Dynasties (3rd to 6th centuries) was re-introduced. The calligraphy leaders of the Meiji period (1868–1912) completely immersed themselves in this "long-lost" calligraphy—probably because it was an extraordinary collection never before seen in Japan, and because it provided an alternative to the "official" style and tradition of the now-discredited previous political regime, the Tokugawa Shogunate.[2]

In Japan's headlong rush to modernize after 1868, calligraphy—unlike other art forms—seemed impervious to influences from the West. During the ultra-nationalistic 1930s there was one tentative effort to create a new calligraphy. While this call for a calligraphy that reflected the changing times was eminently in line with centuries-old traditions, it also implicitly accepted the idea of considering Western approaches, which was a new and dangerous element in such politically tense times. Nothing momentous came of it then, but this call laid the groundwork for major experiments in and a new flowering of calligraphic art after 1945. A basically static situation persisted until 1945, because during this brief period calligraphy was mobilized—as were all other aspects of life and the arts in Japan—exclusively for Imperial purposes.

By mid-1945, like everyone else in post-World War II Japan, calligraphers were faced with shattered ideals and an urgent need to reconstruct. They needed to rethink their old systems, philosophies and assumptions. In their first attempts to rebuild, they tried to create an all-inclusive calligraphy organization and, importantly, incorporated the concept of calligraphic "beauty" and art into its title, "*Nihon Shodo Bijutsuin.*"

In 1948, after political maneuvering, calligraphy was included as the fifth department in Japan's annual national arts exhibition. Thus, for the first time, calligraphy was formally accorded its rightful place among the arts. In 1949, because of calligraphy's earlier association with Imperial objectives, the U.S. Occupation banned the teaching of calligraphy in Japanese schools. As might be expected, this ban was later rescinded by the Japanese government and, despite challenges, calligraphy has been taught in Japanese schools as a required course ever since. As Japan recovered and prospered, calligraphy grew more popular. An ever increasing number of enthusiasts and practitioners, a substantial book-publishing industry, hundreds of calligraphic school journals, over 400 calligraphy exhibitions per year and the burgeoning supply and scroll-making industries signalled the golden age of calligraphy in Japan.

Calligraphy was traditionally the domain of the cultured literati. A person was known for his beautiful calligraphic hand as a politician, a military leader, a poet, a novelist—not as a professional calligrapher. Japan is probably the only country that has published a seven-volume compilation of calligraphies by such leaders.[2] But as times have changed, the impact of the pen and pencil has reduced the need for everyday use of the brush, and the professional calligrapher has come to dominate the calligraphic art world. Still, calligraphy remains a popular and highly respected skill. It is literally part of Japanese spirituality and psychology. The event most symbolic of calligraphy's status is the annual gathering in which thousands of children write their first calligraphy for the New Year at the Martial Arts building next to the Imperial Palace in Tokyo. And yet, there seems among the younger generation to be a creeping sense of ambivalence as to the relevance of this ancient art. This is understandable in light of the pressures on the young to master the intricacies of high-tech society for their survival. Even so, Japan's younger generation continues to study and practice the traditional art of calligraphy.

THE ROOTS OF THE
AVANT-GARDE CALLIGRAPHY
MOVEMENT IN JAPAN.
For centuries there was constant tension and competition between Chinese-leaning and Japanese-leaning calligraphers. From the close encounter with Western abstract art in the postwar period, a third group emerged, those whose calligraphies reflected the influence of Western abstract art with a classic Chinese overlay.[3] This group consisted mainly of the avant-garde. Their creativity had a meteoric rise for some decades but has since levelled off.[4]

The roots of Japanese avant-garde calligraphy must be sought in the 1930s, amid the pre-World War II maelstrom of ultranationalism. Tenrai Hidai, as a disciple of Meikaku Kusakabe (a leading pillar of Meiji calligraphy), studied from among the more than 10,000 Chinese classics that had been brought to Japan in 1881 by Yang Shoujing.

In 1930 Hidai formed an organization to publish these texts and admonished his students that calligraphy could not coexist with drift and pedantry. In 1933 he went further, forming the *Shodo Geijutsusha* (The Calligraphy Art Association) with his disciples and calling for reappraisal of traditional calligraphic values and consideration of incorporating Western ideas and concepts of beauty. In 1937 Hidai was the first calligrapher elected to the Imperial Arts Academy. After his death in 1939, Hidai's disciples continued to demand the rethinking of calligraphy. They suggested that titles for calligraphic art should stem from the feelings of the artist rather than rely on the classics; that characters could be drawn in a variety of unconventional ways; and that works adapting light and dark sumi ink should be accepted. These ideas

HIDAI NANKOKU
1950
Lightning Variation

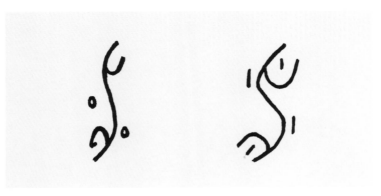

may appear mundane enough, but they were far from conventional in calligraphic terms. Such controlled and limited questioning and experimentation continued throughout the war years, until, in mid-1945, Japan's defeat confronted calligraphers with the collapse of their spiritual foundation.

When World War II ended in August 1945, Nankoku Hidai anxiously reflected on the future of calligraphy in war-ravaged Japan. It was natural that he be concerned with the art's future: a calligrapher himself, he was also the son of Tenrai Hidai. Nankoku's reflections were not particularly fruitful until he recalled his father's admonition to return to the Chinese classics. He then lighted upon *Guzhou Huibian* and was inspired by the ancient character for *lightning*.[5]

In order to show how this ideogram has evolved, the ancient character for *lightning* from the *Guzhou Huibian* is illustrated above together with Nankoku's 1945 rendition, several variations, including the presently used character for lightning, and an Henri Michaux creation (on the following page).

This comparison demonstrates how Japanese calligraphers look to history for inspiration toward the future.

In the summer of 1945, Nankoku went on to create what is now regarded as the first Japanese avant-garde calligraphy. He was so apprehensive as to whether it would be accepted or ridiculed that he entered it in a Western modern art exhibition (Tokyo, March 1946). It was instantly acclaimed. Thus Japan's vigorous avant-garde calligraphy movement (also referred to as sumi-expressionist art, or *bokusho*) was launched.

In 1951 *Bokubi* ("the beauty of black ink [sumi]") was founded. This outstanding journal of experimental calligraphy was published for almost forty years, and it was in *Bokubi* that noted artist Hasegawa Saburo introduced Franz Kline's 1950 paintings. Saburo's 1951 essay included photographs of Kline's work, and—by showing how their culture's ancient calligraphic traditions had been adapted by a renowned Western abstract artist—inspired younger calligraphers to create a new calligraphy by exercising the artistic potential

inherent in traditional calligraphic forms.[6]

Some of the young calligraphers in this new adventure—such as Gatai Osawa, Otei Kaneko, Yukei Teshima, Sokyu Ueda and Nankoku Hidai—became the leaders of the avant-garde calligraphy movement in the decades after the war. (Otei Kaneko, for example, received some of Japan's highest awards in the arts.) These artists introduced the idea of drawing modern poetry instead of relying on the Chinese classics. They felt that the public was neither sufficiently patient nor adequately acquainted with these classics to appreciate them. Instead of long columns of characters, the artists advocated using a few characters drawn with verve and strength. They used lacquer, acrylic and enamel paints and drew not only on paper but also on boards and old rubbings. Through these and many other ingenious and somewhat outrageous means of expression, they quickly departed from merely drawing characters and created non-character calligraphies, semi-abstractions.

THE RELATIONSHIP BETWEEN WESTERN ABSTRACT ART AND JAPANESE AVANT-GARDE CALLIGRAPHY. By the early 1950s, an exchange between Japanese calligraphy and Western abstract art was clearly taking place: newspaper companies (*Yomiuri Shimbun* and *Mainichi Shimbun*) sponsored Japanese exhibitions of modern Western art; New York's Museum of Modern Art exhibited works by nearly 40 Japanese calligraphers; and *Bokubi* (August 1953) published a comparative presentation of works by these Japanese calligraphers and four Western artists.[7]

The evolving relationship between Western abstract art and Japanese calligraphy can be viewed in successive phases: the initial tentative encounter with another culture; the exchange of philosophies, approaches and styles between Japanese calligraphers and Western artists; direct personal interaction among artists; calligraphy exhibitions in the West; and academic and public interest in Japanese calligraphy in the West.

The first phase began with Western interest in Oriental (primarily Chinese) calligraphy after World War I. It was a one-sided fascination with the use, flow and potential of the Oriental brush, recalling the initial Japanese encounter with Chinese calligraphy. Before the West discovered the Oriental brush, a wave of Japanese influence reached the shores of the West in the latter half of the 19th century. It was during this period that European painters encountered Japanese woodblock prints and became preoccupied with abstraction.[8] Meanwhile, in the United States, as Barbara Rose suggests, Transcendentalism, "a major American religion or philosophy[,] essentially synthesize[d] Christianity and Buddhism."[9] Thus the impact of Japanese calligraphy on the Abstract Expressionists could be described as the second wave of Japanese artistic influence to reach the shores of the West. In the 1940s Western Abstract Expressionists developed "a sense that Western ideas, particularly the belief in progress, had been discredited by the events of World War II."[10] Such questioning led to a renewed and deepened appreciation of Oriental philosophy. Western artists' fascination with Zen Buddhism in the 1940s, 1950s and 1960s increased their appreciation of Japanese calligraphy, from which stemmed the Abstract Expressionists' fondness for black-and-white drawings.[11]

The second phase of the relationship between Japanese calligraphy and Western art began when the first exhibition of Japanese calligraphy to be held in the United States after World War II opened at New York's Museum of Modern Art in March 1953. It was followed by another exhibition in 1954 of works by about forty Japanese sumi-expressionists. Since then, more than twenty exhibitions involving Japanese calligraphy have been held throughout the U.S. and Europe (as many exhibitions of Chinese calligraphy have been held as well).[12] While still far outnumbered by those of Oriental painting. these increasingly frequent exhibitions of calligraphy are significant in light of history and past interest. Meanwhile, in Japan there have been many exhibitions on Western abstract art and its impact on Japanese calligraphy.

Japanese avant-garde calligraphy was shown on an equal basis with

Western art for the first time when Yuichi Inoue and Yukei Teshima were invited to participate in the fourth São Paulo Bienal in 1957. In 1958, these two calligraphers were invited to participate in the Brussels International Exposition's exhibition on fifty years of modern art. Teshima was given the highest award for his calligraphy. Thus Japanese calligraphy finally attained world recognition in the arts. Since then, Japanese calligraphers have continued to participate in national and international exhibitions in the West. Moreover, the acquisition by Western museums of works by a number of modern Japanese calligraphers further indicates the increase in international acknowledgment of Oriental calligraphy. Toko Shinoda's creations, for example, are in the collections of museums in the Netherlands, the United States and Germany.

In 1955, Belgian artist Pierre Alechinsky travelled to Japan and created a film on calligraphy.[13] The first instances of Japanese calligraphers in direct contact with the West were Shiryu Morita's journey to Brussels in 1954 and Yukei Teshima's to West Germany in 1955. Subsequently,

Japanese calligraphers—not just the avant-garde group but many of the more conservative traditionalists as well—travelled to Europe, the United States, Australia and South America to explain the fine points of the calligraphic tradition. Feted by their hosts, these artists were impressed with the level of Western interest in their modern renditions of an ancient art. They lectured and demonstrated at public museums, universities and galleries, fostering appreciation of Japanese calligraphy. Most of Japan's senior calligraphers have travelled around the world during the last forty years. Many but not all are avant-garde calligraphers. Shinzan Kamijo, for example, is a fairly traditional calligrapher, yet his strong modern renditions of the classics have great appeal for Western artistic sensibilities.

Another measure of Western interest in calligraphy is the number of books and articles, both popular and academic, and the number of doctoral dissertations written by Westerners about Japanese and Chinese calligraphy. In the late 1980s, there were, surprisingly, over three hundred such books and articles extant, most of which had been published since 1945. Though

still small in number, there was a growing group of adventuresome scholars who chose to study the intricacies of Oriental calligraphy for their doctoral theses.[14]

JAPANESE CALLIGRAPHY TODAY. In the decades after 1945, Japanese calligraphy blossomed into almost a "super-life" in comparison with the previous 1,200 years. In response to the devastation of the 1945 defeat and exposure to Western abstract art, the ancient art of calligraphy was recreated several times over, so to speak, ultimately flowering in avant-garde sumi-expressionism.

Although Japanese calligraphy's interaction with the West has gradually lost its momentum, this interaction has had impact on even the most traditionalistic calligraphy groups. They have been forced to reassess their adherence to the past and have created calligraphies with a distinct modernist tinge, but always within the context of the classics.

Like painting, calligraphy is now largely the domain of the professional and the committed layman. Even though calligraphy schools have flourished, senior calligraphers have commanded large commissions, and the "calligraphy population" is still estimated to number fifteen to sixteen million, it is difficult to gauge the interest of the general populace.

The pendulum has swung away from the more extreme avant-garde calligraphic styles, and traditionalists are under severe and constant pressure from critics to create "a new calligraphy befitting a new age" without any hint of guidelines for this purpose. As an ancient and vital tradition, calligraphy must respond to the challenge as to its worth and validity in a high technology society. So far it has not only survived such challenges, but has thrived.

The works in this exhibition illustrate Japanese calligraphy's continuing struggle to integrate ancient traditions with Western influence, to create an art that is true to the past and relevant to the present.

A calligrapher himself, Cecil H. Uyehara has exhibited his work in several cities and has authored articles and a bibliographic study on Japanese calligraphy. He served as consultant and catalogue editor for "Words in Motion," the Yomiuri Shimbun 's 1984 exhibition of contemporary Japanese calligraphy at Washington's Library of Congress. Uyehara has presented calligraphy lecture-demonstrations at the Smithsonian Institution and at various American colleges and galleries. Uyehara is also a consultant in U.S.-Japan science and technology affairs in Washington, D.C.

NOTES

[1] While most writings on Oriental calligraphy discuss this special relationship, a recent publication that devotes considerable space to this issue is *Words and Images: Chinese Poetry, Calligraphy and Painting* by Alfreda Murck and Wen C. Fong (Princeton University Press, 1991).

[2] Koresawa, Kyozo, et al, compilers, *Sho to Jinbutsu [Calligraphy and People]* (Japan: Mainichi Shimbunsha, 1977-78) v. 7. This series covers the calligraphy of Emperors/Empresses, priests/monks, military/political leaders, scholars, literary figures, and fine artists.

[3] The possibility of this categorization is mentioned by Sugawara Norio in *Gendai no Shoryu* (Japan: Yomiuri Shimbunsha, 1987) 190-191.

[4] Additional background on Japanese calligraphy can be obtained from: Stephen Addiss, "The Role of Calligraphy in Japanese Society," *Words in Motion: Modern Japanese Calligraphy* (Tokyo: Yomiuri Shimbun, 1984), 30-37; Cecil H. Uyehara, *The Rite of Japanese Calligraphy and the Modern Age*, Oriental Art (Summer 1987), 174-182; and two essays on sumi-impressionists by Hariu Ichiro and Amano Kazuo in *Sho to kaiga to no atsuki jidai, 1945-1969, (1992)*—see note 8.

[5] *Guzhou Huibian* is the Pinyin transliteration; the Wades-Giles equivalent is *Ku Chou Hui Pien*. This book was compiled by Hsu Wen-ching and published in 1934. A copy is available in the Chinese Section, Library of Congress, Washington, DC. In Japanese, lightning is *inazuma*, in Chinese it is *dian* (Pinyin) or *tien* (Wade Giles).

[6] This encounter is described in Barbara Rose, "Japanese Calligraphy and American Abstract Expressionism," *Words in Motion.* See also Pierre Alechinsky's "Japanese Calligraphy and Abstraction," *Graphis*, 12 (11-12/56:542-53).

[7] A major retrospective exhibition was held January 2 - February 26, 1992 at the O Art Museum (*O Bijutsukan*) in Osaki, Tokyo on the close relationship and interaction between Japanese calligraphers and painters and Western abstract artists from 1945 to 1969. The calligraphers represented included: Shiryu Morita, Gakyu Osawa, Yuichi Inoue, Yukei Teshima, Toko Shinoda, and Nankoku Hidai. Some of the Japanese painters were: Insho Domoto, Minoru Kawabata, Kenzo Okada, Kokuta Suga, Kumi Sugai, Yasukazu Tabuchi, Teiji Takai, Waichi Tsukata, Misao Yokoyama, and Jiro Yoshihara. The Western artists represented were: Pierre Alechinsky, Gerard Schneider, Hans Hartung, Pierre Soulages, L. Alcopley, Robert Motherwell, Georges Mathieu, Henri Michaux, and Joan Miro. The catalogue, *Sho to Kaiga to no atsuki jidai, 1945-1969 (The time of close interaction between calligraphy and painting, 1945-1969)*, contains two essays by Hariu Ichiro and Amano Kazuo on this relationship and a detailed parallel chronology and bibliography.

[8] This initial influence in the 19th century was the focus of the exhibition, "Seeking the Floating World: The Japanese Spirit in Turn-of-the-century French Art," and was examined in Phylis Floyd's essay in this exhibition's catalog. This exhibition toured Japan and the United States in 1991-1992. Its last stop was at the Meridian International House in Washington, DC.

[9] op. cit., note 5, Rose, 38.

[10] ibid., 39.

[11] See David Clarke's essay in this catalogue for an analysis of the impact of Japanese calligraphy on Western art since 1945.

[12] For more details on exhibitions, see Cecil H. Uyehara, *Japanese Calligraphy: A Bibliographic Study* (University Press of America, 1991) 22-25.

[13] op cit., note 8, 12.

[14] op. cit., note 12. For information on how Japanese scholars and calligraphers view the interaction of calligraphy and Western abstract art, see issues 11 (Fall 1977), 43 (1989) and 49 (1991) of *Sho no Bi (The Beauty of Calligraphy)* which first began publication in 1951. The journal is edited by Mitsuho Arita.

THE CALLIGRAPHIC SPIRIT AND MODERN AMERICAN ART

BY DAVID CLARKE

Since the end of World War II, many American artists have found inspiration in the brushwork of East Asia. The calligraphy of China and Japan, as well as the calligraphic spirit of the great painting traditions of these two nations, significantly influenced the gestural tendency in modern American painting—that is, the tendency to produce images made up of marks that insist upon their status as marks, as records of bodily movement. America's interest in the brushstroke as a spontaneously produced trace probably originated in the paintings of Mark Tobey, an artist who responded deeply to the art and thought of East Asia. Gesturalism was not in full flower, however, until the era of the Abstract Expressionist artists, many of whom were inspired by calligraphy. Although later American artists often rejected Abstract Expressionist gesturalism in favor of cooler images with more impersonal surfaces, the calligraphic impulse has persisted. Brice Marden, who formerly produced paintings in the most reductive of Minimalist idioms, has turned more recently toward calligraphic gesture. His case, perhaps better than any other, illustrates both a strong desire for evidence of the human touch in art, and the continuing relevance of East Asian brushwork to the concerns of American artists.

For the most part, American art inspired by East Asian brushwork is not directly comparable in visual appearance to anything Chinese or Japanese. In such works, not mere formal mimicry but an encounter with an alternative world view takes place. Calligraphy has functioned as a material channel through which American artists have encountered complex notions of East Asian aesthetics and metaphysics. Tobey described how calligraphy played such a role for him after one of the lessons in Oriental brushwork he received from Teng Gui in 1920's Seattle.[1] "I came out and I saw a tree and the tree was no longer a solid"—the dynamic linearity of the Chinese calligraphic gesture had given him an intimation of the Buddhist and Taoist world view.[2]

The full impact that Tobey's encounter with East Asian modes of understanding had for his paintings took some time to become clear. In 1934 he traveled to China and Japan, deepening his knowledge of the art of the brush. While staying with Teng Gui in Shanghai, Tobey continued his study of calligraphic brushwork as a formal discipline at a local art school.[3] In Japan he did much the same, and was encouraged to interpret calligraphic marks in the philosophical context of Zen Buddhism. While staying at a Zen monastery, he was given an *enso* (a freehand-brushed circle) on which to meditate, and in his discussions with Soetsu Yanagi (whom he described as being interested in his brush drawings and very knowledgeable about art) Tobey claimed to have been given many ideas about Zen.[4]

Tobey also encountered calligraphy in more mundane contexts during his East Asian trip. For instance, in a letter from Shanghai, Tobey wrote about "the language, the beautiful character writing," probably referring to the signs that lined the streets rather than to calligraphy as an art practice.[5] Tobey again referred to this sign-writing when he described the dynamic life of Shanghai:

Thousands of Chinese characters are twisting and turning, in every door is a shop. The rickshaws jostle the vendors, their backs hung with incredible loads. The whole scene is alive in a way Broadway isn't alive...the human energy spills itself into multiple forms, writhes, sweats, and strains every muscle towards the day's bowl of rice.[6]

"Chinese characters...twisting and turning" describes movement of human as well as calligraphic figures—as if Tobey was, with the double meaning of the word "character," giving himself a verbal cue as to how he should represent such an animated scene. Urban dynamism is the subject of ensuing Tobey works, such as *Broadway Norm* (1935), in which a linear vocabulary indebted to Tobey's study of East Asian brushwork is evident. "The calligraphic impulse I received in China enabled me to convey, without being bound to forms, the motion of people and cars and the whole vitality of the scene."[7]

When Tobey described "writing a picture" as opposed to "building it up in the Renaissance tradition," he not only indicated his familiarity with the traditional East Asian conception of painting and calligraphy as closely related activities, but also showed the priority that line came to have for him as a result of his study of calligraphy.[8] Using it as a resource, Tobey attempted to "demolish form," which he saw as an element commonly over-emphasized in Western art.[9] In resulting works such as *Written over the Plains, No. 2* (1959), a new cosmology—rather than merely a new stylistic emphasis—is present.[10]

The sculptor Ibram Lassaw, who shares Tobey's deep interest in East Asian art, explicitly proposes such a connection between stylistics and cosmology. For Lassaw, "the Greco-Roman idealistic philosophy is one of static, eternal truths, perfection," producing sculpture that "tends to be static and monolithic, a closed system."[11] Lassaw's sculpture, by contrast, evidences an approach closer to East Asian metaphysics, taking for a basic assumption the idea of reality as process and relationship as opposed to solid permanent mass. His works, such as

The Clouds of Magellan (1953), provide three-dimensional parallels to Tobey's paintings in their dynamic linearity and interconnectedness of elements.

For Tobey, East Asian calligraphy provided an introduction to gestural modes of painting. The same was not necessarily the case for most artists of the Abstract Expressionist generation, acquainted as they were with Surrealist automatism. Surrealists saw this practice—analogous to Freud's employment of free association in the clinical situation—as a means of overcoming rational intention, of releasing the creativity of the unconscious, and for Surrealist theorist André Breton, a goal in itself.[12]

Surrealist automatism and East Asian calligraphy are directly linked in the thinking of Theodoros Stamos, who has referred to "the expressive glory of Chinese calligraphic characters."[13] In a 1950 discussion with other artists, Stamos asked whether automatic painting is conscious or not, pointing out that in the early 1900s Ernest Fenellosa wrote an essay on the Chinese character as a medium

in poetry: "Are artists today familiar with it [Stamos continued], or are such characters or writing unconscious? There is an amazing connection between the two."[14] The question of the extent to which the Surrealist automatist gesture was conscious arose for Stamos because what matters to him in Oriental art is "the concentration of thought and the prompt and vigorous action of the hand to the direct will." Stamos feels that East Asian brushwork, unlike unconscious doodling, requires "an infallible technique."[15]

An interest in Oriental calligraphy can also be documented in the case of Robert Motherwell, and was an apparent factor in his espousal of what he described as plastic automatism (as opposed to Surrealist psychic automatism). When Motherwell talked of calligraphy he emphasized the issue of spontaneity, of moving beyond conscious intention in a way that recalls Surrealist concerns.

You learn from Japanese calligraphy to let the hand take over: then you begin to watch the hand as though it is not yours, but as though it is someone else's hand, and begin to watch it critically. I find myself making it jump more, or making it become more rhythmic, or making it drive off the edge at a certain moment; that is a whole different way of drawing compared to looking at something and marking its shapes down . . . if it is exactly right, my hand just flies and I do not even have to think; my hand just does it, as though I am not there.[16]

Motherwell wanted to retain—even in such a large-scale work as *Reconciliation Elegy* (1978)—"the immediacy of . . . Oriental calligraphy." Indeed, in two 1977 sketches for this painting he used a Japanese brush.[17]

Motherwell seemed to appreciate the autonomy of line in East Asian calligraphy—in his own paintings, line is given freedom

from descriptive tasks, from the burden of suggesting boundaries to three-dimensional forms. The resulting dynamic energy can be seen in many of his works, but the parallels with calligraphy are particularly noteworthy in works, such as *Gesture Paper Painting No. 22* (1975), in which the linear elements assemble, without losing their discrete identities, into character-like forms. Motherwell's frequent reduction of means to black gestural marks on a white surface further reinforces the parallel with calligraphy. The artist himself acknowledged a specific affinity between his understanding of black and its use in East Asian art. Motherwell conceived of black as a hue, an idea he considered to be "most rare, except in Japan."[18]

With Motherwell, as with Tobey, calligraphy seems to have been the bearer of a novel world view. In Motherwell's case it is the use of empty space in East Asian calligraphy—most fully developed by the Japanese—that intimates the

ISAMU NOGUCHI
1969
Magic Rng
RED PERSIAN TRAVERTINE
96 X 7-7/8 INCHES

Buddhist notion of the void. As Motherwell made clear, he wished to give his own images a similar metaphorical allusion to that which he perceived in East Asian art. He saw his *Open* series, in particular, as "built on a conception analogous to the Oriental conception of the absolute void: that you start with empty space, and that the subject is that which animates the great space, the void. The amazing discovery is that it takes relatively lit-

tle to animate the absolute void."[19]

In an untitled monotype of 1987, Motherwell produced a variation on Sengai's *Circle, Triangle and Square*. That Motherwell chose this particular image for his most direct attempt to parallel an East Asian precedent is not surprising, since, unlike the characters which make up the Chinese and Japanese scripts, geometric forms have meaning in a Western context. Motherwell fought against the language barrier more

than any other American artist, seemingly dissatisfied that a Western response to Oriental calligraphy could be made only within painting and not in writing. This fight is exemplified by Motherwell works that take letters of the alphabet as their subject, such as *A, No. 2* (1968) or *Q* (1968). Letters, unlike words, have a unitary structure analogous to that of characters, and presenting letters in isolation removes their referential meaning and thus makes them more like characters. Spontaneity of execution and an awareness of negative space relate these images to works by such Japanese calligraphers as Jiun[20] and Nantembo[21] who both employed the splashed ink effects Motherwell favored in works such as *Samurai IV* (1974).[22]

The very unintelligibility of Chinese and Japanese characters to most of the American artists who encountered them may sometimes have enhanced their appeal. This was true for Seymour Lipton, who demonstrated that sculptors also found sustenance in this Eastern art form. Lipton said that *Sentinel* (1959) "stems directly from a Chinese written symbol of which I have no knowledge at all . . . .The form and meaning . . . emerged from my own private experience, but the original stimulus was the Chinese writing which mysteriously appeals to me."[23] The final appearance of *Sentinel* bears traces of Lipton's interest in Chinese characters in its language of linear elements, some of which have a broadening at their ends analogous to that found in certain strokes used in Chinese writing—

particularly that which employs the standard script (*kaishu*). The dynamic conception of compositional structure that Lipton favored in this work also relates to his study of the forms of Chinese characters. The same is true of Herbert Ferber's *Calligraph with Wall* (1957), but any conscious link between this sculpture and East Asian writing systems was *post facto*: "I called these works calligraphs because they resemble calligraphy, but the similarity was recognized after I made them from my drawings, which I also realized resemble calligraphy."[24]

Isamu Noguchi also took an interest in calligraphy as a resource for sculpture. While it hardly seems surprising that a Japanese-American should look to such a highly regarded East Asian art form for inspiration, the incomprehensibility of calligraphy to a Western audience presented Noguchi with the same challenge that other American artists faced. Like Motherwell, Noguchi bypassed the problem of language by turning to Sengai's *Circle, Triangle, and Square*. This famous piece—also the model for Belgian

artist Pierre Alechinsky's *Variations after Sengai* (1960)—was undoubtedly the inspiration behind Noguchi's *Beinecke Rare Book and Manuscript Library Garden* (Yale University, 1960–64), which contains a circle, a pyramid and a cube. Instead of an ideal Platonic form, Noguchi's sculpture court features a pierced circular element with slight asymmetries and imperfections, such as those the free brush marks introduce into the Sengai piece.[25] In both works a greater sense of dynamism is the consequence.

Describing some connotations of the pierced circular form in his Beinecke Garden, Noguchi claimed that "the circle is zero, the decimal zero or the zero of nothingness from which we come, to which we return. The hole is the abyss, the mirror, or the question mark."[26] He was alluding to the Buddhist notion of the void; the space enclosed by the stone takes on the role played by the bare white canvas for Motherwell. Other Noguchi works that also employ empty space in circular forms to evoke metaphysical connotations include: *Energy Void*

BRICE MARDEN
1988–89
Diagramed Couplet
OIL/LINEN
84 X 40 INCHES

23

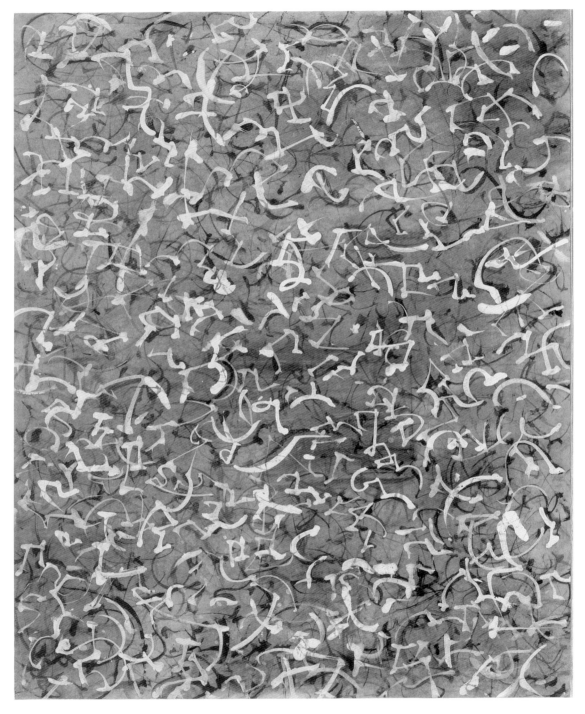

MARK TOBEY
1978
Written Over the Plains, No. 2
GOUACHE ON PAPER
12 7/16 X 9 3/4 IN

(1971), *The Void* (1970) and *Magic Ring* (1969). In these works, empty space is given an even more prominent role than in the *Beinecke* circle. *Magic Ring* in particular evidences that calligraphy suggested the means whereby abstract philosophical notions might be embodied in the concrete form of an art work. The incomplete circle of this work recalls the freehand *ensos* that were drawn by Jiun, Torei, Bankei and various Zen calligraphers for use in Buddhist practice. The eccentrically shaped and often discontinuous circles in these images also inspired Paul Jenkins. His *Magic Circle* (1955), for instance, demonstrates how such calligraphic images can evade language barriers and enter Western art.

Stone may seem a particularly unresponsive medium in which to parallel something as spontaneous as Japanese calligraphy. Indeed, Noguchi lamented that sculpture is so bound by inertia. In some of his later works Noguchi engineered massive splits in the stones to produce shapes that could not have been predicted. Although they bear no visual resemblance to calligraphy, these works nevertheless aspire to the spontaneity so valued in Zen brushwork. Noguchi used the rather Zen-sounding term "sudden awareness" to describe the innocent frame of mind wherein inspiration comes unwilled.[27] Although he believed it was possible for a sophisticated modern artist to attain this state of mind, Noguchi felt that Hakuin's greatness as a calligrapher was a consequence of his being an untrained amateur, a Zen monk rather than an artist.

Such interest in Zen was not peculiar to Noguchi. Many American artists of the post-1945 period gave Zen their attention, and it is easy to see why it appealed to them. As artist John Ferren stated when recalling that "everyone [in the New York art world] was interested in Zen in the '40s and '50s," Zen had for them "an element of spontaneity in it, and was anti-intellectual, and that was part of the temper of the time."[28] It is important to note the extent of Zen's popularity, because it was largely in a Zen context that East Asian calligraphy was interpreted in the United States.[29] The focus tended to be on Japanese calligraphy, with Zen-associated artists such as Sengai, Hakuin and Jiun being perhaps the most highly valued. Chinese calligraphy, and those aspects of the Japanese tradition that are not so Zen-inspired, were often either passed over or misconstrued. Some of the most distinctive calligraphy to be produced in Japan, for instance, is that which uses the native *kana*, rather than *kanji* (characters borrowed from the Chinese written language). But since Zen tended to favor *kanji*, calligraphy written in *kana* was not as closely scrutinized by the Abstract Expressionists.

Gesturalism became a widespread tendency in American painting as a consequence of the success of Abstract Expressionism, and almost inevitably, this led to a reaction. The Hard-Edge, Minimalist and Pop painting movements that followed eliminated all traces of the artist's touch in favor of a cool, impersonal finish. Artists as diverse as Frank Stella, Ellsworth Kelly and Roy Lichtenstein all seem to have set themselves against spontaneity, creating an artistic climate in which the influence of Oriental calligraphy was unlikely to prosper. Yet many Minimalist artists have been as inspired by East Asian philosophic notions as their gestural predecessors were. This is true of Agnes Martin and Carl Andre, for instance, and the late near-monochrome works of Ad Reinhardt—such as *Black Painting* (1960–65)—are as deeply concerned with the Buddhist concept of the void as Motherwell's Open series was.[30] Although they have no look of calligraphy (unlike certain works Reinhardt produced in the 1940s), gesture still played a role in the creation of these paintings. In visual parallel to a Buddhist meditation process, Reinhardt used gestures to cancel out one another, leading to a state where all traces of individuality are erased—the "empty," near-monochrome canvas is a corollary to *samadhi*, the Zen or Buddhist state of mental self-absorption in which the ego is transcended.

The resurgence of Expressionist painting in the 1980s demonstrates the difficulty of keeping gestural traces out of painting for long. Even artists associated with

Minimalism have forsaken the reductive surfaces of their earlier works in favor of a new gesturalism. Foremost among these is Brice Marden. In Marden's recent works, monochrome fields have been replaced by linear networks that are indebted to his study of Chinese calligraphy and painting. Marden acknowledges this Eastern influence in his titles—the title of the *Cold Mountain* sequence refers to the Tang dynasty Han Shan poetry collection, while *Diagramed Couplet* refers directly to calligraphy: in East Asian calligraphy a couplet is a unit of verse in two successive lines presented on a pair of vertical hanging scrolls; in *Diagramed Couplet (No. 1)* (1988–89) gray and green calligraphic gestures are rhythmically arranged in two parallel vertical columns against a bare white backdrop. However abstract, *Couplet*'s predominantly gray forms (which were apparently executed first) are analogous to a sequence of characters. The green lines (added later) serve to link these "characters" horizontally as well as vertically and suggest the way the Asian eye might move in order to take in a couplet. "There's a different reading than we get in Western poetry," Marden observed.[31] The manner in which Marden executed the *Couplet* works further parallels Eastern practice: following the traditional pattern of Chinese and Japanese writing, Marden began at the top right and worked downward.

Marden's *Couplet* series shows that it is still possible for a Western artist to find a new way of responding to East Asian calligraphy. As their needs change, Western artists will undoubtedly be able to find further resources in the Chinese and Japanese art of writing. The process of interpretation can never be finished, and in the case of Oriental calligraphy in the West, it may have only just begun.

David Clarke did his doctoral study at the Courtauld Institute, University of London, and now teaches in the Department of Fine Arts at the University of Hong Kong. The primary focus of his research has been American art, although he is now also writing about the response of East Asian artists to Western Modernism.

NOTES

[1] I am using pinyin romanization here. Teng Gui normally chose to romanize his name as "Teng Kuei." He also signed himself in Chinese as "Bai ye."

[2] Mark Tobey, in interview with William Seitz, tape III, side 1, transcript p. 40, Seitz Papers, Archives of American Art.

[3] Tobey sent examples of his calligraphy from Shanghai to Dorothy and Leonard Elmhirst with a letter, dated May 3, 1934 (Dartington Hall Archives, Devon, England), stating: "enclosed is a sample of my own Chinese writing which my friend [Teng Gui] says belongs in three years practice grade."

[4] Tobey describes this experience in "Japanese Traditions and American Art," *College Art Journal* XVIII (1958): 24: "Day after day I would look at it. Was it selflessness? Was it the Universe—where I could lose my identity? Perhaps I didn't see its aesthetic and missed the fine points of the brush which to a trained Oriental eye would reveal much about the character of the man who painted it. But after my visit I found I had new eyes and that which seemed of little importance became magnified in words, and considerations not based on my former vision." In the same essay Tobey also writes (p. 22) of "the circle of emptiness freed by the imagination" which "permitted one to reach a state of mind which released one from having to consider someone else's ideas." Tobey's interest in Zen

Buddhism was renewed in the later 1950's, partly through the influence of his Seattle friend, Takizaki. Indeed, Zen ink traces are more closely recalled by the Sumi works he produced in 1957, such as *Space Ritual, No. 1* (Seattle Art Museum), than by any of his other images.

[5] Mark Tobey, letter to Dorothy Elmhirst, dated April 25, 1934, (Elmhirst Papers, Dartington Hall Archives).

[6] Mark Tobey, "Reminiscences and Reveries," *Magazine of Art* 44 (Oct. 1951): 230.

[7] Mark Tobey, quoted in William Seitz, *Mark Tobey* (New York: Museum of Modern Art, 1962) 51. Although the modern city street may seem a long way from the refined world of the traditional calligraphic artist, it

should be noted that Tobey's friend, Teng Gui, gave a lecture in which he "dealt with lines, comparing them to all types of human beings, some muscular and powerful and abrupt, and others showing signs of decadence." ["Expressionism in Chinese Art: Chinese Authority's Address to Local Club," *The North-China Herald* CXC (Shanghai, Jan. 31, 1934) 172]. Even Tang dynasty calligrapher Zhang Xu was supposedly inspired by an altercation witnessed in the street (see Jean Francois Billeter, *The Chinese Art of Writing* (Geneva: Skira, 1990) 177.

8 Mark Tobey, quoted in Katherine Kuh, *The Artist's Voice* (New York: Harper and Row, 1963) 236.

9 Mark Tobey, in an interview with William Seitz, quoted in F. Hoffman, "Mark Tobey's Paintings of New York," *Artforum* 17 (April 1979) 25.

10 Tobey's linearity is inspired by Oriental calligraphy, but does not always bear a detailed resemblance to it. In *Written over the Plains*, No. 2 (in the collection of the Seattle Art Museum) however, there are specific similarities between his brush strokes and those found in calligraphy. There is nothing in this image, though, that is an equivalent to a full character, and one may conjecture that this response to calligraphy at a level below that of the semantic unit is more likely in the case of someone who does not have a real appreciation of the meaning of characters.

11 Ibram Lassaw, undated printed note, Lassaw papers, Archives of American Art.

12 See David Clarke, *The Influence of Oriental Thought on Postwar American Painting and Sculpture* (New York: Garland, 1988) esp. 52-57 for further discussion of Surrealism's debts to the Far East.

13 Theodoros Stamos, quoted in Kenneth B. Sawyer, *Stamos* (Paris: Georges Fall, 1960) 23.

14 Theodoros Stamos, April 23, 1950, at the third "Artists' Sessions at Studio 35," in R. Motherwell and A. Reinhardt eds., *Modern Artists in America* (New York: Wittenborn, Schultz, 1951) 20.

15 Theodoros Stamos, 1954 lecture "Why Nature in Art," quoted in Barbara Cavaliere, "Theodoros Stamos in Perspective," *Arts* 52 (December 1977) 112. Stamos is using, almost unchanged, the words of Georges Duthuit's 1936 study *Chinese Mysticism and Modern Painting* (London: Zwemmer), which draws parallels between Far Eastern philosophical tenets and Surrealist practice. Duthuit was the son-in-law of Matisse, and knew both Joan Miro and Andre Masson. All three of these artists are discussed in the text. The same passage by Duthuit is also quoted in Daisetz T. Suzuki's *Zen and Japanese Culture* (Princeton: Princeton University Press, 1959) 31. When Stanton Macdonald-Wright discusses calligraphy, he, like

Stamos, emphasizes the degree of control involved. Macdonald-Wright studied Chinese calligraphy for more than a decade and felt that there was a quality of line in his painting that was indebted to the Tang and Song Chinese calligraphy.

16 Robert Motherwell, quoted in J.D. Flam, "With Robert Motherwell," *Robert Motherwell* (New York, Abbeville, 1983) 23.

17 Robert Motherwell, quoted in E.A. Carmean ed., *Robert Motherwell: The Reconciliation Elegy* (Geneva and New York: Skira/Rizzoli, 1980) 68. In a telephone conversation with the author (December 29, 1979), Motherwell pointed out that more than a mere look of spontaneity was at stake. He stated that (in relation to his Open series) it was important to him that the gestural marks were spontaneously executed, even though deliberately made marks might appear no different.

18 Robert Motherwell, quoted in Stephanie Terenzio, *Robert Motherwell and Black* (Connecticut: William Benton Museum of Art, 1980) 81. Motherwell noted that Matisse also has a sense of black as hue, but only conjectured that he may have learned it from Oriental calligraphy.

19 Flam, p.23. Motherwell said (in a telephone conversation with the author, December 29, 1979) that his interest in Zen was largely a development of the 1960s, and it is consistent with this fact that his earlier works do not always have such an unbounded sense of space: in *Elegy to the Spanish Republic No. 34* (1953–54), for instance, the white areas function more as part of a basically two-dimensional image that is contained compositionally within the boundaries of the framing edge. The same is true of Franz Kline's paintings, which have nevertheless frequently been compared to Oriental calligraphy.

20 Jiun's *The Sanskrit Letter A* (Kinami Collection) offers an example of a Far Eastern calligrapher applying calligraphic brushwork to an alien writing system.

21 Nantembo is further comparable to Motherwell in that he attempted calligraphy on the same large scale that the Abstract Expressionists favored. See, for instance, Stephen Addiss, *The Art of Zen: Paintings and Calligraphy by Japanese Monks, 1600-1925* (New York: Harry N. Abrams, 1989) 192-4. Nantembo's work was featured in *La Calligraphie Japonaise*, a film that Belgian painter Pierre Alechinsky made during his 1955 visit to Japan. Although there is not space to consider it here, it should be noted that European gesturalist artists' interest in East Asian calligraphy broadly parallels that of their American counterparts.

22 Motherwell's choice of title for his *Samurai* series was consistent with his view that Oriental calligraphy offered a resource for counteracting the decorative ten-

dency in Abstract Expressionist brushwork. Discussing his Je t'aime series, he stated that it was "a gesture of anger at the increasing tendency towards decorative surface in the development of American avant-garde painting in the mid-1950s, and a manifesto for a return to what the ancient Chinese call 'The Spirit of the Brush' [the title of a 1939 book by Shiho Sakanishi that Motherwell and William Baziotes read in the 1940s]." [H. H. Arnason, *Robert Motherwell* (New York: Harry N. Abrams, 1982) 130.] There is even an ancient Chinese treatise on painting called (to my eternal reassurance) "The Battle Formations of the Brush." David Smith also emphasizes what he sees as the forceful quality of Japanese calligraphy, which influenced his own two-dimensional work: "Certain Japanese formalities seem close to me, such as the beginning of a stroke outside the paper continuing through the drawing space, to project beyond, so that in the included part it possesses both the power of the origin and the projection. This produces the impression of strength." [Smith, quoted in Paul Cummings, *David Smith: The Drawings* (New York: Whitney Museum of American Art, 1979) 26.] Smith was particularly interested in Japanese *reisho* style calligraphy and his ex-wife, Dorothy Dehner, recalls experiments with Oriental brushes taking place at Smith's Bolton Landing studio (telephone conversation with the author, July 8, 1980).

23 Seymour Lipton, letter to the author, April 26, 1980, in which Lipton emphasized that "most important to me visually has been my absorption in Chinese calligraphy."

24 Herbert Ferber, letter to the author, July 6, 1980.

25 Suzuki, p. 24, "one of the favorite tricks of Japanese artists" has been to "embody beauty in a form of imperfection or even of ugliness." Concerning Suzuki's influence on American artists, see Clarke, pp. 79-83.

26 Isamu Noguchi, undated printed note, Artist's file, Whitney Museum, New York.

27 Isamu Noguchi, conversation with the author, June 18, 1980.

28 John Ferren, interview with Paul Cummings, June 7, 1968, transcript p. 42, Archives of American Art. Ferren dates his own first contact with Zen to the 1920s.

29 For further information on the popularity of Zen in American artistic circles, see Clarke, op. cit. note 12.

30 For further information on Reinhardt, Andre and Martin's interest in Oriental thought see Clarke, op. cit. note 12.

31 Brice Marden, in Robert Mahoney, "Brice Marden: This is What Things Are About," *Flash Art* (International Edition) 155 (Nov./Dec. 1990) 117.

THE HISTORY AND PRESENT STATUS OF JAPANESE CALLIGRAPHY

BY ICHIRO HARIU

THE PLACE OF CALLIGRAPHY IN MODERN JAPAN. Like all art forms, the spirit of calligraphy originates from the identity and sensitivity of its creator. Each work reflects the artist's varying interpretation of animating blank paper with eloquent line. The basic technical conditions for the creation of a work of calligraphy are the angle of the writing brush, the pressure exerted on the brush and the speed of writing. All of these variables affect the quality of line and the structure of the characters. When it originated in China, calligraphy was considered an important element of culture and a skill that every member of society should acquire; it was considered one of the "six arts," along with etiquette, music, archery, horsemanship and arithmetic. Chinese *kanji* are hieroglyphic, ideographic characters that were probably produced by the abstraction of basic pictorial symbols.

In Japan, in addition to *kanji* borrowed from China, phonetic characters called *kana* were produced from parts of the *kanji* and a more simplified writing style. This led to the development of both a rectilinear, orderly *kanji* calligraphy and a curvilinear, flowing *kana* calligraphy.

Calligraphy and painting are similar in that they are produced by brush and ink or paint, and often a person who is a superior calligrapher is also a great artist. The art forms of poetry, calligraphy and painting became fused into one.

However, it was not until the 1870s, just after Japan emerged from its long feudal period, that calligraphy began to gain recognition as a significant art form in its own right. In 1872 encyclopedist and Western scholar Nishi Amane delivered lectures on aesthetics to the Emperor Meiji that argued that since drawing, sculpture, woodblock prints and architecture, (as well as literature, music, dance, and theater) seek beauty, they were called "the fine arts" in the West; but in China, calligraphy should also be included. At that time, traditional Japanese arts and crafts including calligraphy won high praise when exhibited for the first time at the Vienna World's Fair. As a result, the Agriculture and Commerce Ministry of Japan presented calligraphy, sculpture, woodblock prints, photographs and industrial arts as the main exhibition categories at domestic industrial expositions in 1877 and 1881. However, calligraphy's recognition as an art form remained tenuous.

The School of Industrial Arts opened in 1876, and the Japanese government invited three instructors from Italy to introduce Western techniques such as oil painting, carving and modeling, geometry and the laws of perspective to the curriculum. Traditional Japanese arts including calligraphy were excluded from the school. Landscape artist Foutenage, one of the invited instructors, was popular among the students, but became ill with beriberi and returned to Italy after only two years. As a result of his absence and reductions of school funding, many students collectively withdrew. The government, meanwhile shifted away from Europeanism toward ultranationalism, and abolished the school in 1883.

The year before, oil painter Shotaro Koyama, former student of the School of Industrial Arts, proclaimed in a magazine that "calligraphy does not constitute art." He reasoned that calligraphy consists of symbols for language and that, as one must write characters of fixed form, it would never constitute art. In response, Tenshin Okakura, an official at the Ministry of Education, countered that although calligraphy certainly possessed the practical aspect of language, if the diverse modulations in calligraphic style expressed inner ideas and gave pleasure to people, it became art. In 1888 the Tokyo School of Fine Arts opened. In 1889 Okakura was promoted from manager to school director, and the curriculum was restricted to traditional arts and crafts such as Japanese painting, wood carving, metalwork and lacquer work. Calligraphy was excluded along with oil painting, Western carving and modeling, and copperplate printing. Therefore, it was clear that Okakura did not attach much importance to calligraphy, but rather championed the revival of traditional art forms that would reflect the ultranationalism of the time.

Okakura, who was a high government official and a disciple of professors at Tokyo University, invited artists Seiki Kuroda and Keiichiro Kume, who had also returned from France, to be professors at the university. A Western painting department was thus established at this school, but calligraphy remained excluded.

From the perspectives of both modernism and traditionalism, the old doctrine of the "union of calligraphy and painting" was shattered, and traditional and oil painting were structured into the curriculum of art schools as the two genres of painting. Calligraphy was entrusted to primary school education, with emphasis on its practical aspects.

In tracing the evolution of calligraphy, one finds in 1880 a jolt to the tepid calligraphic style of the late Edo period: the introduction of over 10,000 reprints of ancient Chinese master calligraphers brought to Japan when Chinese historian Shoujing Yang joined the Chinese embassy. During the long period of national isolation, there had been no opportunity in Japan to study the evolution of Chinese calligraphy. Access to this collection marked the first time that the Japanese were presented with the stone monument inscriptions of the Northern Wei region, dating before the Tang dynasty. Meikaku Kusakabe and Ichiroku Iwaya, government officials who had also studied Chinese poetry and prose, approached Shoujing Yang to view the collection and became ardent admirers of the powerful style.

In 1911 the Chinese Manchu dynasty was overthrown. Many scholars of Chinese classics sought refuge in Japan. Partly because of their influence, Chinese literary research and Oriental history became more deeply rooted in Japan. As a result, calligraphy as an expression of spirituality lessened, and works were cut off from literature and scholarship; calligraphy lapsed into mere technical competition.

At this same time, however, calligraphy as a hobby spread to an ever-larger segment of society, and a proliferation of calligraphy schools, group exhibitions and calligraphy magazines were established. The classical practice of copying characters from a model book was no longer used, and only the example written by the teacher was imitated. Thus, calligraphy became a populist hobby.

In 1930, however, Tenrai Hidai

took measures to reverse this trend in establishing the Calligraphy Institute. He constantly urged his students to return to the Chinese classics and sought a free and unconventional creativity based on an awareness of the "art of the lines." In 1933 the elite pupils of Tenrai Hidai (including Sokyu Ueda, Yukimura Uno, Gakyu and Chikutai Osawa, Sofu Okabe, Otei Kaneko, Kazan Samejima, Yukei Teshima, and Hidai's son Nankoku) formed the Calligraphic Art Association. The students challenged the established value system of calligraphy, conducting an ongoing debate concerning the introduction of Western aesthetic concepts. In 1937, two years before his death, Tenrai Hidai gathered pupils and notables from the world of calligraphy to form a public organization, the Great Japan Calligraphy Institute.

In 1940 Sokyu Ueda dissolved the Calligraphic Art Association and founded the Keiseikai Club. A year later, he brought together unconventional calligraphers, including the Tenrai Hidai group, to organize the Calligraphy Reform Council. The council caused an uproar in the calligraphy world during World War II by experimenting with stippled patterns using dark ink and soft brushes made of wool, the use of light inks which until then had been considered taboo as "calligraphy in mourning," and the scattered writing of *kanji*. The council also proposed to make the title of a calligraphic work depend not on the original classical source but on the inspiration of the calligrapher.

Immediately after Japan's defeat in World War II, when reforms against long-established custom marked a crisis in traditional art, it was mainly the Tenrai Hidai group that pioneered changes in calligraphy.

NEW APPROACHES TO
CALLIGRAPHY AND PICTORIAL
ART AND THE ESTABLISHMENT
OF AVANT-GARDE
CALLIGRAPHY. In late 1945, in an attempt to organize a coalition of calligraphers amid the postwar crisis, the Japan Calligraphy Art Academy was established with Saishu Onoe as chairman and Shunkai Bundo and Gakukshin Isono as vice-chairmen. In 1948, as a result of the long negotiations of Shunkei Ijima and Otei Kaneko, the Mainichi Newspaper Company established the Mainichi Calligraphy Exhibition as a general exhibition of calligraphic works. Also, the Japan Arts Academy (Nitten) Exhibition (a reincarnation of the Government exhibition that had been criticized as a stronghold of state regulation of the arts and collaboration with the war effort) established the Calligraphy Division as its fifth category in 1948. Based on instructions from American occupation forces, it was reinstated that year as an incorporated entity, separate from the national budget.

These two exhibitions were considered proof that calligraphy had finally received social recognition as an art form. Yet this acceptance was not necessarily a result of the initiative of calligraphers nor praise for their work. That this occured at a time of great change in the system of government reflected the endorsement of the newspaper companies and the Nitten Exhibition toward the energy of calligraphy. At the request of Shunkai Bundo, the Tenrai Hidai group also participated in these exhibitions as judges and officers, but the revolutionary experiments in calligraphy occurred away from these sites.

For example, Nankoku Hidai, who had inherited the publishing business of the Calligraphy Institute and served during the war in the Land Survey Department of the General Staff Office, was forced to escape to a mountain village in Nagano Prefecture where his sister and her husband lived. That autumn, as Hidai studied the ancient Chinese Classics (prompted by his dying father's instructions to "return to the past when one reaches an impasse"), he was suddenly inspired by the Chinese character "den" (lightning). As a result he was soon attempting a form of abstract expressionism, which he named "heart line works." These works were exhibited at the Modern Art Exhibition of 1946, where considerable controversy arose as to whether they were really calligraphic works. Their innovative style, however, inspired a number of calligraphers to search for new direction.

In 1947 Sokyu Ueda, Sesson Uno, Gakyu Osawa, Chikutai Osawa, Suiken Suzuki, Yukei Teshima and Shiryu Morita founded the Calligraphy Art Institute. After grad-uating from the Printing and Industrial Arts Course of the Tokyo School of Industrial Arts Nankoku Hidai established the Yokohama Seihan Research Institute, and also revived the *hihaku* calligraphic style of classical China to apply it to his abstract works. In Kyoto, Shiryu Morita launched a correspondence-course publication (*The Beauty of Calligraphy*) in 1948 with Sokaku Ueda as editor-in-chief. While in Takasaki, Gakyu Osawa sponsored *Shogen*, issued the same year by the Heigen Corporation. These publications served as the official mouthpieces of the Keiseisai and the Calligraphic Art Institute, respectively. Morita deepened his friendship with abstract painter Saburo Hasegawa (who came from the same Hyogo Prefecture). In autumn 1949 Morita established a new department in *The Beauty of Calligraphy* that solicited public contributions of experimental works including paintings, which were selected and evaluated by Hasegawa. In 1951 a second publi-cation, *Bokubi* (Ink Beauty*)*, was issued, which emphasized the rela-tionship between calligraphy and modern painting.

In 1952 Morita joined with Yuichi Inoue, Sogen Eguchi, Taihei Sekiya and Rissi Nakamura, and the artists separated from the Keiseikai and the Calligraphy Art Institute and founded the Bokujin Club, which promoted more avant-garde experimentation. In 1950 Untei Akabane, Suiken Suzuki, Kakusen Tsugane,Yukie Teshima and Ko Hirao had left the Calligraphic Art Institute to form the Japan Calligraphic Works Institute, but it quickly broke up, dividing into the Independent Calligraphy Club (Yukei Teshima, Taiku Tokuno and Taiho Yamazaki) and the Kairankei (Suzuki, Tsugane and Hirao). That year, Sofu Okabe, Suijo Ikeda and Ryuho Kobayashi also withdrew from the Calligraphic Art Institute and formed the Sojinkai.

Behind this rapid proliferation of small groups was the fact that while these artists originally partic-ipated in the Nitten Exhibition and the Mainichi Calligraphy Exhibition under the premise of a coalition, they also used the Calligraphic Art Institute as a base for avant-garde experiments, and the contradiction of this dual purpose became too difficult to ignore. Master calligrapher Sokyu Ueda aroused much public criticism at the 1951 Nitten Exhibition by exhibiting the one-character calligraphic work of *hin*, (items) which appeared as three scattered pieces of rock entitled *love*. In 1953 Gakkyu Osawa's posthumous work *Black Hell, Black Valley* was made in the style of the painter Shiko Munakata whom he greatly admired. Because it featured symbolic writing arranged on a background of scattered points of light ink, it was denied display at the Nitten Exhibition despite the fact that it was an invitational exhibit. As a result, Sokyu Ueda withdrew from the Nitten Exhibition in 1955, and Sesson Uno followed in 1956.

Another underlying element in this duality was international exchange, which had been blocked during the initial period of the occupation as it had been during the war and rapidly intensified just before the conclusion of the peace treaty. After World War I, geometric abstractionism and Surrealism fused in a variety of ways beginning in the 1930s, ultimately converging in the work of Abstract Expressionists, many of whom developed an interest in Oriental calligraphy.

In 1950 Japanese-American sculptor Isamu Noguchi visited Japan, homeland of his father, poet Beijiro Noguchi, to open a private exhibition. He observed that in all likelihood the only escape from the impasse of Western civilization lay in the traditional culture of the Orient. Saburo Hasegawa, who studied art history at Tokyo University, studied abroad in Europe and progressed into abstract works, and then became devoted to traditional Oriental art including calligraphy during World War II, was troubled by the postwar gap between traditionalism and modernism. He confessed: "The moment I met Mr. Noguchi, this distress disappeared, and I felt as if a great road had been opened before my eyes." And it was not only Hasegawa. Painters like Hiroya Abe, Genichiro Inokuma, Kenzo Okada, Minoru Kawabata and Tadashi Sato, who served as members of the Army Press Corps during the war and who felt guilty for having drawn propagandistic war paintings, were influenced greatly by their encounters with Noguchi and soon went to live in Europe and America.

Also in 1950, the modern works of 100 European and American artists were exhibited at the "Modern World Art Exhibition" sponsored by the Yomiuri Newspaper Company. The works of American painters, including Roberto Matta and Mark Tobey (who was inspired by calligraphy during his voyage through China and Japan in the 1930s), Jackson Pollock, Clyfford Still, Mark Rothko, Theodoros Stamos and Ad Reinhardt were represented, as well as works by the circle of the Salon de Mai of France including calligraphic painters such as Pierre Soulages, Gerard Schneider and Hans Hartung. The exhibition evoked little response, but among Japanese critics of the time (as may be expected), the French works were considered to be highly refined, while the American works were viewed as coarse and lacking spatial sense.

The "Salon de Mai Japan Exhibition," sponsored by the Mainichi Newspaper Company in 1951, further intensified this reaction and was hailed as a synthesis of modernism and the return to tradition that had emerged from the resistance movements under the wartime occupation of the German army. Later, however, the eclectic character of this salon was recognized. Ironically, among the Osaka group of abstractionist artists who collaborated on *Ink Beauty*, only Jiro Yoshiwara who later organized the "Concrete" group, pointed out the refreshing attraction of American art.

In his *Stray Thoughts on the New West and the Old East*, which was serialized in publications from *The Beauty of Calligraphy* to *Ink Beauty* in 1951, Saburo Hasegawa touched on his impressions of the "Salon de Mai Japan Exhibition," his correspondence with Tal Coa, a devotee of Taoism, and the photographs of works of Franz Kline that were brought by Isamu Noguchi on his second postwar trip to Japan. He writes:

> Calligraphy and pictorial art should be united. Two thousand years of Oriental tradition teach us this, and today, here and there throughout the world, earnest young new artists are throwing themselves body and soul into this enterprise . . . Perception of formative properties was heightened by paintings subsequent to Cézanne; this purification progressed with the rise of abstractionist painting; and today the eyes of the progressive artists of Europe and America are turned with wonder and ardor toward the calligraphic art of the East.

The overseas exhibitions of Japanese calligraphy began with the "Modern Calligraphy Exhibition" at the Museum of Modern Art, New York, in September 1952. Twenty-five works from the Calligraphy Art Institute by calligraphers Suijo Ikeda, Manri Imai, Chikutai Osawa, Sofu Okabe, Shunran Kagawa, Kankyo Ukai, Ryuho Kobayashi, Toko Shinoda and Sofu Takeshi were included. In 1953, the "Japanese Architecture and Calligraphy Exhibition" also opened at the museum, and 36 artists were featured, including Yuichi Inoue, Sokyu Ueda, Sesson Uno, Sogen Eguchi, Gakyu Osawa, Gaboku Ogawa, Kumo Shiritsu, Shunran Kagawa, Bakusan Sakaki, Toko Shinoda, Sofu Takeshi, Futoshi Tsuj and Shiryu Morita. In 1955 exhibitions of the Bokujinkai were held in Paris and Brussels, in which European artists who had previously corresponded with Koryu Morita (including Pierre Soulages, Gerard Schneider, Raoul Ubac, Camile Bryen, Alcopley, Pierre Alechinsky, Michel Souphore, William Hayter and Corneille) also cooperated and exhibited.

In autumn 1955 "Modern Japanese Calligraphy—The Art of Ink" opened at the Tokyo National Modern Art Museum, with 105 works by 81 calligraphers which then toured Europe through autumn of the following year. In 1957 the Keiseikai also began a traveling exhibition in the U.S. of 25 works by Sokyu Ueda, Sesson Uno, Gaboku Ogawa and Bakusan Sakaki. Meanwhile, when Belgian painter Pierre Alechinsky came to Japan to open a private exhibition, he also produced a documentary film on avant-garde calligraphy.

The ideological leaders of the Bokujinkai were Buddhist philosopher Shinichi Hisamatsu and aesthetician Tsutomu Ijima, both Kyoto University professors. Ijima was sent overseas by the

Education Ministry, and while conducting research in Paris saw the "Modern Japanese Calligraphy" exhibition. Guided by Alechinsky, he visited critic and painter Michel Souphore, who was deeply interested in calligraphy. According to a report (*Ink Beauty*, 1956, vol. 8) by Shigenobu Kimura who acted as an interpreter, Souphore praised the exhibition and said that several Japanese calligraphers had been included in a recently published abstract art encyclopedia; yet Ijima noted that it was rather one-dimensional to view calligraphy as abstract painting. Souphore commented there was no essential difference between the abstractionist rendering of a tree by Mondrian and the abstraction of calligraphy that departs from its literal basis. Ijima responded that calligraphy was artistic expression based on everyday communication, and that while calligraphers were free to depart from the letter or character and move toward picture drawing, one could not deny that there was also adherence to the character.

During this period, the drawings and letters of Souphore, Corneille,

Camile Bryen, Jack Cox, Alechinsky, Franz Kline and René Robie were introduced in *Ink Beauty*. In 1956 the "World Contemporary Art Exhibition" sponsored by the Asahi Newspaper Company assembled representative works of the post-World War II artistic currents of European "Informel" and American Abstract Expressionism, and the relationship between calligraphy and painting was more deeply explored.

Poet and art critic Shuzo Takiguchi wrote in "The Calligraphy of East and West" (*Ink Beauty*, 1957, vol. 1):

> When one compares the contemporary calligraphy of Western Europe with that of China and Japan, one finds that while the latter began by conforming to the symbol of the written character and recently has given birth to expression which denies the character, Western European calligraphy never developed the concept that the written style of the letters was artistic expression, but rather has sought to arrive at calligraphy by seeking unknown symbols from among paintings . . . Yet, in many of the works of the Bokujinkai, one feels that more than the horizontal lines it is the vertical impacts which constitute the main operative force, and that the strokes are more expressive as a result of this force which seems to explode forth after being pent up inside. Furthermore, in works with titles such as *Kutsu* (Cavern) by Mr. Sogen Eguchi, *Hitsuzen* (Necessity) by Mr. Ikuo Deguchi, and *Shakunetsu* (Scorching Heat) by Mr. Koryu Morita, the formative feel of the characters themselves is somewhere dimly present. These titles may in some cases have been given afterwards, but one nevertheless feels that the relation to the characters has not been severed... But what I have found odd is that the works of several artists overly resemble each other . . . Various formats can be observed amid the developments in the new calligraphy of today, but it would appear that, to an unexpected degree, quite constrained work is continuing within the confines of conventional formats.

In 1977 Michel Tapie, a leading critic of the Informel, came to Japan in the company of painters George Mathieu, Sam Francis and

Toshimitsu Imai. Tapie gave lectures and contributed to newspapers and magazines, while the painters conducted private exhibitions and production demonstrations. This resulted in an Informel "group style." Thereafter, Tapie frequently visited the museums, galleries and ateliers of Japan. From the "Concrete group" to Japanese painters Insho Domoto and Hidetaka Ono to *ikebana* (flower arrangement) master Sofu Teshigawara, Tapie unearthed works that he then sent to overseas exhibitions, but avant-garde calligraphy works were not among them.

In 1958 Soulage and the Chinese painter Wou Ki Zao (who resided in France) arrived in Japan, and held a round-table discussion with Shiryu Morita at the offices of *Ink Beauty*. Shuzo Takiguchi and earlier painter Jiro Yoshiwara were unable to rid themselves of dissatisfaction with the avant-garde calligraphy that was being discussed in the publication. This was undoubtedly because of their belief that when calligraphy was separated from the characters, its internal energy and sense of life was dissipated. It approached

Expressionism and Fauvism, going beyond these into unknown signals and spatial consciousness.

It is true that Japanese calligraphy enjoyed great popularity overseas, and at meetings to select Japanese works for the international exhibitions of this period, I would hear requests from the sponsoring countries that we include avant-garde calligraphy. Therefore, Yuichi Inoue and Yukei Teshima joined the ranks of the exhibiting artists at the 1957 São Paulo Bienal, and were invited to the "50 Years of Modern Art" exhibition at the 1958 Brussels World's Fair. The same year, Sokyu Ueda and Shiryu Morita were invited to the Carnegie International Exhibition in Pittsburgh. In 1959 "Tradition and Innovation in Japanese Art" at the Claire Mueller Art Museum in Holland featured Edo-period calligraphic and pictorial art works of the Zen monk Hakuin (1685-1768), as well as the modern woodblock prints by Shiko Munakata and calligraphic works by Toko Shinoda and Nankoku Hidai. Meanwhile, Yuichi Inoue, Yukei Teshima and Taiho Yamazaki were invited to the

Documenta II exhibition in Kassel, Germany.

In 1960 works by Yuichi Inoue, Sokyu Ueda, Sesson Uno, Yukei Teshima, Nankoku Hidai and Shiryu Morita were exhibited at a calligraphy exhibition in Freiburg, Germany. In 1961 the works of 28 artists appeared in the "Japanese Calligraphy" exhibition that toured Germany, while Sokyu Ueda and Sesson Uno participated in the São Paolo Bienal and Yuichi Inoue, Toko Shinoda and Koryu Morita were invited to the Carnegie International Exhibition. In 1963 28 artists were invited to the "Meaning and Symbols" exhibition that toured Germany; Toko Shinoda, Nankoku Hidai and Shiryu Morita participated in the "Japanese Ink Drawing Exhibition" that toured America; Yukei Teshima participated in the 21st Century Exhibition in Seattle, Washington; and Toko Shinoda exhibited at the Carnegie International Exhibition. The same year, works of the Edo period and by Suijo Ikeda, Yuichi Inoue, Sokyu Ueda, Sogei Eguchi, Yukei Teshima, Yasushi Nishikawa, Nankoku Hidai, Joryu Matsui and

Shiryu Morita were exhibited at the "Calligraphy and Figures Exhibition" in Amsterdam and Baden-Baden, while 10 artists participated in the "Modern Japanese Calligraphy Exhibition" that toured Australia. In 1964 works of Sofu Okabe, Nankoku Hidai and Shiryu Morita were exhibited in the "Modern Japanese Painting Exhibition" that toured America.

In light of these developments, it was only natural that the American critic, Jules Langsner, should harbor questions after coming to Japan and seeing "Masterworks of Modern Japan," the art exhibition at the 1964 Tokyo Olympics. Langsner found that while the conventional classifications of "Western painting" and "Japanese painting" were followed, calligraphy was completely excluded.

> Curiously, this exhibition excludes calligraphy, which is one of the most contemporary of traditional East Asian arts with regard to its spiritual nature, its morphological and spatial concepts, and its vibrant sense of life. Thanks to the many representative artists of calligraphy, it is presently undergoing remark-

ably creative innovations in Japan. In practice, the refusal to exhibit the works of avant-garde calligraphers of first-class ability—beginning with Nankoku Hidai, Shiryu Morita, and Sofu Okabe—signifies that the sponsors attach no value to the intermingling of the traditional art of China and Japan and the modern art of America and Europe (*The Yomiuri Newspaper*, October 23, 1964).

Yet in retrospect, this period was the peak of foreign interest in calligraphy. By the late 1960s, though there were still exhibitions of Yuichi Inoue, Toko Shinoda, Nankoku Hidai and Shiryu Morita in Europe and America, group exhibitions by Yukei Teshima and his group and invitations to various artists to participate in international exhibitions, the number of survey exhibitions of calligraphy sponsored by Western art museums markedly diminished. First, the main current of modern art was moving away from Abstract Expressionism, which is close to calligraphy, toward incorporating duplications or reproductions of reality (as in Pop art and hyperreal-

ism), and toward seeking direct links between the material and the conceptual and discarding all types of depiction and interior expression (as in minimal art and conceptual art).

Second, along with Japan's industrial development, symbols of Japan as seen from abroad shifted from elements of traditional culture such as Zen, Noh, "restrained elegance," calligraphy and gardens to such products as transistor radios, motorbikes and automobiles. However, a third point is perhaps most important: the avant-garde calligraphy that had separated itself from the written character ultimately proved unable to create new symbols and spatial relations. Since the separation of calligraphy from poetry and painting at the beginning of the modern era, it had lost sight of its spirituality and message, and despite its external prosperity, was unable to surmount the decadence of the technical competition avidly supported by calligraphy schools and organizations. It was indeed symbolic that Shiryu Morita, who through *Ink Beauty* had forged ahead more fervently with avant-garde experiments and international exchange than anyone else, returned to the basis of the characters in 1970, and devoted himself to researching and assuming classical calligraphic methods.

In my view, as avant-garde calligraphers who crossed the boundaries of Fauvism and expressionism, mentioned above, one should cite Nankoku Hidai, Toko Shinoda and Yuichi Inoue, none of whom opened calligraphy schools or sought pupils. During the 1950s, while continuing to study English for purposes of propagating calligraphy abroad, Hidai devoted himself to the exploration of diverse materials and techniques: spreading lacquer on boards, applying water, and then smearing on India ink; or conducting transference by the *hanpon* (a book printed from engraved wooden blocks) method and writing on top of old hanpon; or spreading oil paint over the entire surface of the board and scratching in the *hihaku* calligraphic style with tire fragments.

During the 1960s, while touring America and Europe, and continuing to conduct exhibitions, lectures and the direction of actual artistic production, Hidai reaffirmed that the constitution of calligraphy lies in the pure abstraction derived from lines. Through methods involving mixing black oil paint and benzene, or rubbing and mixing two types of classical Chinese ink and their coagulation, he would paste *tori-no-ko* paper onto veneered board and then prepare and apply a liquid as the undercoating in the same color as the paper. He would then write using classical Chinese ink and apply a final coating of acrylic matte, which gave a solid durability to an expression that was becoming increasingly light and stylistically easy.

Toko Shinoda resided in the U.S. after the late 1950s, where he learned much from the paintings of Abstract Expressionism. As American critic J.J. Sweeney has noted, while adhering to the point of departure for India-ink drawing referred to as "visual poetry and elegant drawing," Shinoda tentatively reached out to wall calligraphy on buildings, ceramic reliefs, folding screens, chisel writing in concrete with steel pen or sword, drop curtains, textile fabrics, and other media, and developed a mode of expression for display which keenly cut through space with flowing lines and gave tension to the negative space.

Yuichi Inoue served as a head teacher and school principal, and continued on as a primary and junior-high school instructor. For a period (inspired by Pollock) he departed from written characters and scrawled on enamel with a broom, but by the end of the 1950s, he had returned to the starting points of characters, writing brush and ink. Yet he rejected solely purposeful structure, and immersed himself in writing hundreds of sheets of one or two or three characters, aiming to give concrete form to space by Dadaist methods that sought the unrestrained vibrancy of life.

Inoue has passed away, but the problems mentioned above continue to weigh heavily on the calligraphy of today. In this exhibition, both works that preserve the basic form of the written characters and works whose characters are illegible at first glance are present in equal proportions; and both forms confront common problems from their respective angles.

Professor Hariu received his BA in 1948 from Tohoku University and his PhD in aesthetics in 1954 from the University of Tokyo. He has been a professor at Tama Art College, and since 1973 has taught at Wako University. He has been active as an art critic throughout his career, and served as Japanese commissioner for the 1968 Venice and 1977 and 1979 São Paolo biennial exhibitions. Hariu has written several books on contemporary art, including: Avant-Garde Art *(1961);* A Diagnosis of Contemporary Art *(1964);* History of Postwar Japanese Art *(1976);* Language and Non-Verbal Language *(1979); and* A Painter of Agony *(1990).*

ELOQUE

NT LINE

林錦洞
直視

KINDŌ HAYASHI
Facing the Truth, Staring at the Truth
INK ON PAPER
85 X 85 CM

This is based on a Buddhist saying about purifying the heart. One of the oldest styles of Chinese characters was used pictorially with a variety of brush pressures and speeds, conveying both strength and enlightenment.

北島瑞峰
鳴

ZUIHŌ KITAJIMA
A Bird's Cry
INK ON PAPER
89 X 89 CM

An unusual rendering of the character
for the bird's cry. The character
consists of a bird and a mouth that
are transformed into the beak and
cockscomb of a bird. This
contemporary version refers back to
the ancient roots of this Chinese
character.

佐々木泰南
壷

TAINAN SASAKI
Jar
INK ON PAPER
86 X 67 CM

A stylized abstract rendition of the character for *jar*.

十鳥霊石
踏舞

REISEKI TOTORI
The Dance
INK ON PAPER
90 X 50 CM

The two characters for *The Dance* appear in the Chinese classics on ceremonies. The intent here is to mark the occasion of this special U.S. exhibition with a joyous message. *The Dance*, a rendering in a black ink with a bluish cast similar to that used in the Ming period in China (1368-1662) emphasizes movement and beauty.

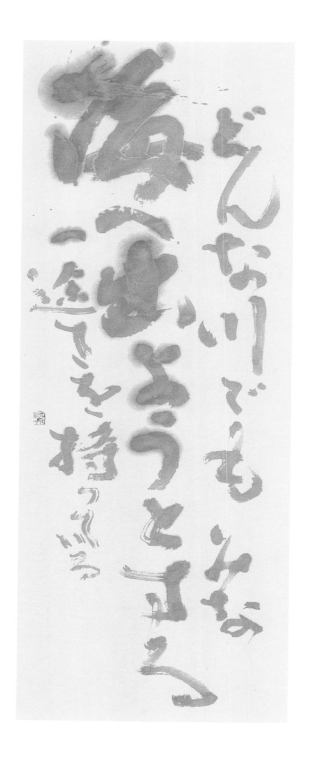

渡辺誠泉
どんな川でもみな海へ

SEISEN WATANABE
Striving Rivers
INK ON PAPER
170 X 71 CM

All rivers strive to reach the ocean;
similarly people also strive to reach
their highest potential.

長島南龍
上

NANRYŪ NAGASHIMA
Above
INK ON PAPER
90 X 90 CM

An impressionistic re-creation of the
simple character meaning "above" or
"to go up". Through varying hues that
range from stark black to fading
grays, a three-dimensional quality is
created.

国井誠海
肅

SEIKAI KUNII
Prudence
INK ON PAPER
137 X 54 CM

A contemporary rendition of a
complicated character that shows the
possibilities of combining line and
shape.

山田松鶴
舞

SHŌKAKU YAMADA
Dance
INK ON PAPER
93 X 48 CM

The line evokes the graceful elegance
of dance. Reflective gold flakes
suggest the play of light on the
dancer's costume. The intent here
was to convey the deliberate yet light
movements of Japanese dance.

小川瓦木
串の幻想

GABOKU OGAWA
An Illusionary Skewer
INK AND GLUE ON PAPER
165 X 53 CM

The character for skewer is
impressionistically created. Gaboku
Ogawa first exhibited at the Museum
of Modern Art, New York in 1953.
Since then he has exhibited
internationally in Europe and North
and South America.

島村谿堂
吉野懐古

KEIDŌ SHIMAMURA
Retrospective on Yoshino
INK ON PAPER
48 X 92 CM

A poem by Yanagawa Seigan that praises the famous *Yoshino sakura* blossoms. The calligrapher's intent is to hope that the cherry blossoms in Washington, D.C., similarly evoke springtime with their annual beauty.

小川南流
安歩以當車

NANRYŪ OGAWA
Accepting Poverty
INK ON PAPER
154 X 50 CM

Translated literally, the characters
mean "walking slowly and changing
vehicles," or accepting poverty
without making any demands.

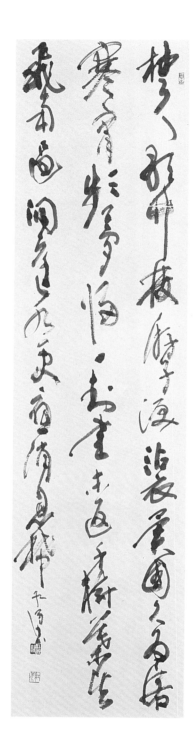

岩田紅洋
干武陵詩

KŌYŌ IWATA
A poem by Yu Wuling
INK ON PAPER
170 X 50 CM

A nostalgic poem about being away from one's home country for some time: "the cold weather makes one dream of returning, the leaves of trees are all gone, news of home is rare."

佐々木鐵仙
古都玲瓏

TESSEN SASAKI
The Old Capital
INK ON PAPER
132 X 70 CM

A calligraphic image of the old
capital of Kyoto. In the upper right
there is an unusual calligraphic seal.

大地無邊礙塵無數我等作罪亦復無數虛
空無邊我等作罪亦復無邊方便無邊我等
作罪亦復無邊法性無邊我等作罪亦復無
邊法界無邊我等作罪亦復無邊眾生無邊
我等劫奪秘害亦復無邊三寶無邊我等侵
損劫奪秘害亦復無邊戒品無邊我等毀犯
亦復無邊如是等罪上至諸菩薩下至緣聞
緣覺兩不能知唯佛與佛乃能知我罪之多
少今於三寶前法界眾生前發露懺悔不敢
覆藏唯願十方三寶法界眾生受我懺悔憶
我清淨始從今日頓首法界眾生捨邪歸正
發菩提心慈心相向佛眼相看菩提眷屬作
真善知識同生阿彌陀佛國乃至成佛如是
善罪永斷相續更不敢作懺悔已至心歸命
阿彌陀佛

錦永正子敬書

廣懺悔文

敬白十方諸佛十二部経讃大菩薩一切賢
聖及一切天龍八部法界衆生現前大衆等
證知我　發露懺悔從無始已未乃至今
身秋害一切三寳師僧父母六親眷屬善知
識法界衆生不可知數偷盗一切三寳師僧
父母六親眷屬善知識法界衆生物不可知
數於一切三寳師僧父母六親眷屬善知識
法界衆生上起邪心不可知數妄語綺誕一
切三寳師僧父母六親眷屬善知識法界衆
生不可知數綺語調咲一切三寳師僧父母
六親眷屬善知識法界衆生不可知數惡口
罵辱誹謗毀呰一切三寳師僧父母六親眷
屬善知識法界衆生不可知數兩舌闘亂破
壞一切三寳師僧父母六親眷屬善知法
界二百五十戒五百戒菩薩三聚戒十無盡
戒

三上錦水
広懺悔文

KINSUI MIKAMI
Buddhist Scripture
INK ON PAPER
60 X 40 CM

Copy of Buddhist scripture from the Pure Land Buddhist group. The drawing/writing of a Buddhist scripture is accepted as a religious experience and helps the writer achieve a religious nirvana.

遠藤乾翠
竹聲松影

KANSUI ENDŌ
The Grove Whispers and Pine Shadows
INK ON PAPER
150 X 60 CM

Bamboo hums as the breeze wanders
through; the moon pursues the
shadow of the pine trees. In each
case, the breeze and moon are not
included, demonstrating the method
of understatement or implied
statement of Japanese poetry.

川上鉌晶
七言二句

TESSHŌ KAWAKAMI
A Calligraphic Poem
INK ON PAPER
172 X 50 CM

Two Chinese poems, consisting of
seven characters are recorded: "The
dew on the chrysanthemum is like a
cool human emotion" and "The frost
is powerful like sake and intoxicates
the red pear leaf."

三宅剣龍
雙翼

KENRYŪ MIYAKE
Two Wings
INK ON PAPER
89 X 87 CM

The imagery of two wings of an
aircraft, which soars splendidly
despite its delicate membranes and
structure.

佐々木月花
満

GEKKA SASAKI
Full
INK ON PAPER
71 X 65 CM

The contemporary rendition of the
character for *full* or *complete*.

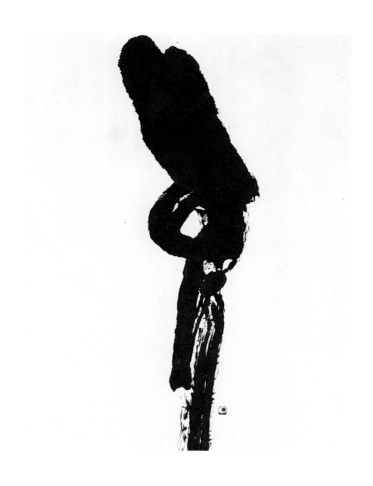

佐野丹丘
祈り

TANKYŪ SANO
Prayer
INK ON PAPER
96 X 83 CM

Through prayer, which is universal,
we strive to attain inner peace, or a
feeling of "oneness" with the world.

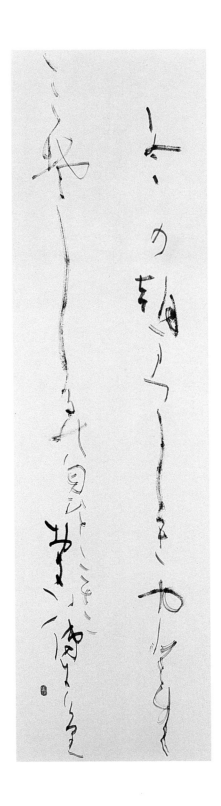

讃岐泰泉
冬の朝

TAISEN SANUKI
A Winter Morning
INK ON PAPER
145 X 51 CM

A poem, drawn in Japanese *kana* syllabary, about waking in the morning to the odor of miso soup.

田中鳳柳
鳥黒鷺白

HŌRYŪ TANAKA
A Study in Black and White
INK ON PAPER
62 X 78 CM

A black crow and a white heron,
rendered in the seal script style.

斎藤香坡
平和の基に世界は今・・

KŌHA SAITŌ
A Poem Dedicated to World Peace
INK ON PAPER
170 X 49 CM

"The world has begun moving, as in a circle based on peace. The United States, as a pillar of this endeavor, is being watched by all countries. Japan is now moving forward in this direction, utilizing its bitter wartime experience in a constructive manner."

本多道子
はじめにひかりがありました

MICHIKO HONDA
In the beginning, there was light
INK ON PAPER
170 X 71 CM

A contemporary use of the Japanese syllabary (*kana*) in shades of gray and bleeding ink, with substantial negative space symbolizes this romantic cosmogony.

村越龍川
嵩壁蘭

RYŪSEN MURAKOSHI
Sūhekiran
INK ON PAPER
169 X 49 CM

Sūhekiran is the title of a poem that describes an artist drawing orchids that are growing on a high, craggy rock. Cheng Hsieh (1693-1765) was an official, a poet, calligrapher, and painter who specialized in painting orchids, bamboo and rocks.

山本宏城
目断天涯

KŌJŌ YAMAMOTO
Beauty Beyond Imagination
INK ON PAPER
217 X 53 CM

The universe of nature is beauty beyond what the eye (the top character) can perceive. This calligraphic style is adapted from ancient Chinese forms.

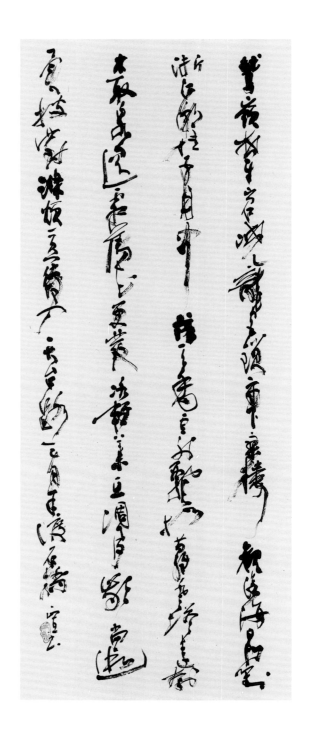

岩田正直
駱賓王詩

MASANAO IWATA
Poem by Lo Binwang
INK ON PAPER
168 X 74 CM

A modern rendition of a seventh
century Chinese poem of 70
characters by Lo Binwang. Lo visited a
temple and lyrically described the
views of the sea, the morning sunrise,
the mountains, and the mystical
ambiance of the temple environs.

金田石城
水雲

SEKIJŌ KANEDA
Watery Clouds
INK ON PAPER
60 X 83 CM

A poetic expression in a contemporary
style of water and clouds.

生田観周
捲土重来

KANSHŪ IKUTA
To Start Anew with Restored Energy
INK ON PAPER
169 X 71 CM

"To err is human, but we must learn from our errors and strive for new success." These four characters are written vigorously as a whole, as one mass.

池田青軒
瑤華

SEIKEN IKEDA
A Brilliant Stone
INK ON PAPER
136 X 72 CM

This is a calligraphy that will mellow
as one watches, studies and
meditates on it.

風岡五城
道在邇

GOJŌ KAZAOKA
The Truth is Nearby
INK ON PAPER
157 X 70 CM

Three strongly rendered characters
emphasize the architectural nature
and the variety of line styles of this
calligraphy. The title derives from an
aphorism by Motze, a Chinese
philosopher of the 4-5th century B.C.

久保田朴仙
風

BOKUSEN KUBOTA
Wind
INK ON PAPER
88 X 72 CM

The wind, which gently moves through
the atmosphere is symbolized by light,
lyrical brush strokes and light shades
of grey.

秋元松風
さくら

SHŌFŪ AKIMOTO
Cherry Blossoms
INK ON PAPER
94 X 49 CM

*Cherry blossoms in the early morning
sunlight* is a combination of the
Japanese syllabary and Chinese
characters. Its changing strokes and
spacial variety convey a sense of
flowery lightness.

柴田侑堂
書藝生涯

YŪDŌ SHIBATA
A Life in the Calligraphic Arts
INK ON PAPER
156 X 50 CM

Two sets of characters denote one's life commitment to the calligraphic arts. At the top are characters for the calligraphic arts. Characters for the individual's life are beneath them.

田中蘆雪
歌

ROSETSU TANAKA
Singing
INK ON PAPER
169 X 49 CM

Singing is a calligraphy about
fondness. Dominated by a large
vigorous character which means "to
sing," the small inscription reads:
"rather than sing by myself, it would
be delightful to hum with you."

岡村翠瑤
葉

SUIYŌ OKAMURA
The Leaf
INK ON PAPER, GLUE AND
ALUM
94 X 48 CM

A fluid rendering suggesting an
autumn leaf.

宮澤静峰
大地

SEIHŌ MIYAZAWA
Living in Pollution
INK ON PAPER
54 X 66 CM

This work is an appeal against the pollution of the earth, which has reached dangerous levels. The calligraphy consists of two characters for universe or the earth; the small character for "big" in the upper right, and the larger one for "ground" is to the left, both rendered in a black, smudged style that suggests pollution.

今口鷺外
龍潜淵

ROGAI IMAGUCHI
The Dragon in the Deep Valley
INK ON PAPER
52 X 95 CM

The dragon — which is the first character on the right — is a legendary sacred figure in East Asia, a felicitous symbol that is representative of large, bold action. The dragon is also the symbol of the Chinese Emperor. Here the dragon is in the valley awaiting the right moment.

遠藤竹泉
春倒梅邊第一風

CHIKUSEN ENDŌ
Spring Winds
INK ON PAPER
156 X 54 CM

A seven character statement in Chinese about the arrival of the plum blossom and the spring winds. The quality of the line varies to reflect the many possibilities of spring.

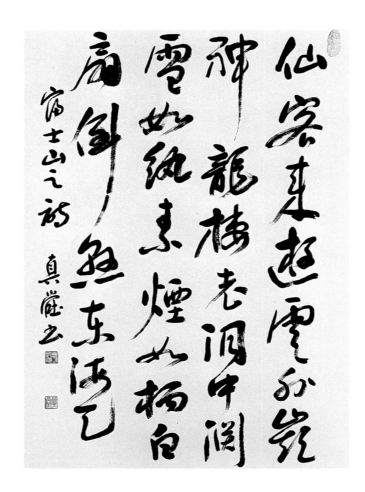

愛澤真堂
富士山

SHINDŌ AIZAWA
Mt. Fuji
INK ON PAPER
112 X 84 CM

A calligraphic rendition of a poem by
Ishikawa Jozan about Mt. Fuji, the
legendary and symbolic mountain
of Japan.

岩浅写心
宇宙からのメッセージ

SHASHIN IWAASA
A Message from Space!
INK ON PAPER USING
JAPANESE PAINTING COLOR
PIGMENTS
96 X 68 CM

This contemporary abstraction
alludes to a man listening for a
message from space.

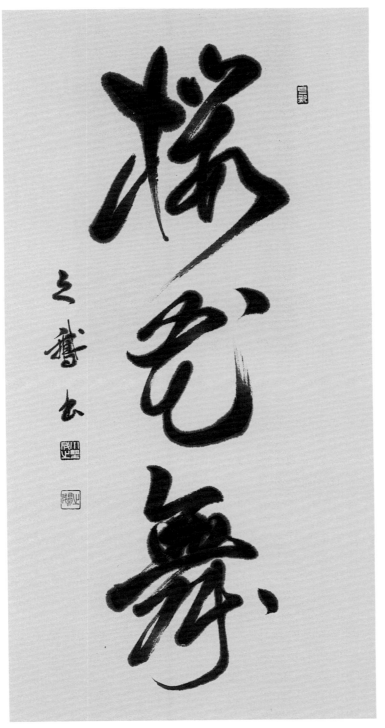

小野之鶩
櫻花舞

SHIGA ONO
Dancing Cherry Blossoms
INK ON PAPER
93 X 48 CM

Dancing Cherry Blossoms was created while the calligrapher was thinking of those famous trees dancing in the spring breeze in Washington, D.C.

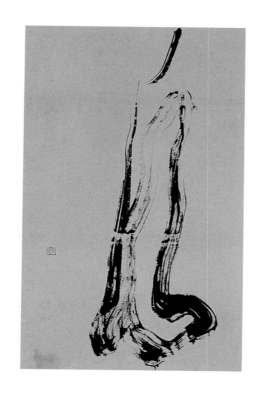

朝比奈玄甫
'92初冬II

GENPO ASAHINA
Early winter 1992
INK, GLUE ON PAPER USING
OSTRICH FEATHERS
93 X 60 CM

The unremarkable, stylized character
"Bon" is rendered lyrical and unusual
with an ostrich feather.

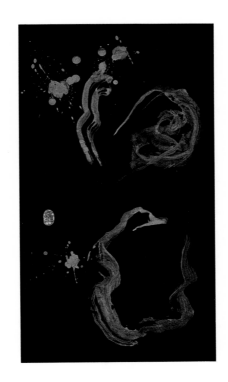

原田圭泉
烟火

KEISEN HARADA
Fireworks
GOLD INK ON PAPER
92 X 51 CM

Vivid fireworks burst against the
black sky.

工藤峰寿
人輪

HŌJYU KUDŌ
Circle of People
INK ON PAPER
55 X 65 CM

A combination of an abstract
character for "people" and a radical
adaptation of the character for "ring"
or "circle."

小林朴翠
鶏鳴一声

BOKUSUI KOBAYASHI
The Year of the Chicken
INK ON PAPER
92 X 48 CM

1993 is the Year of the Chicken, or
Rooster, in the Eastern Zodiac
calendar; (1921, the year the artist
was born was also the Year of the
Chicken). The Rooster is proudly
announcing the arrival of the
New Year.

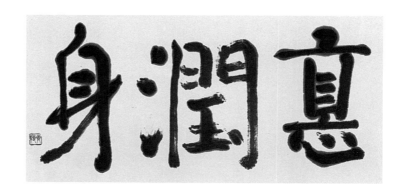

佐藤青苑
徳潤身

SEIEN SATŌ
*Virtue/Goodness is Man's
Greatest Wealth*
INK ON PAPER
52 X 94 CM

A straightforward Zen aphorism is
drawn in standard block script on
special paper that produces a shadow
of the brush stroke.

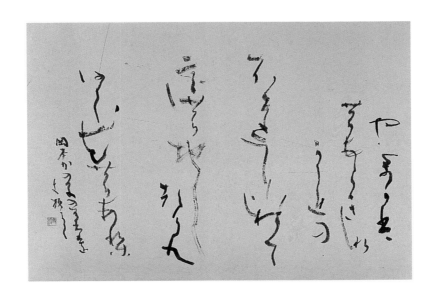

宮本丈梗
やまかわの・・

JŌKŌ MIYAMOTO
Rushing Waters and Life
INK ON PAPER
72 X 100 CM

Rushing mountains streams
Alongside,
A flower quietly blooms

Poet Okamoto Kanako of the Meiji
period (1868-1912) compares the
precarious, challenging lives of
women to those of flowers that cling
desperately to the banks of a rushing
stream.

樋口裕子
妙

HIROKO HIGUCHI
Mystery
INK ON PAPER
148 X 56 CM

The "mystery" character is rendered
in alternating bold and fading lines.

菊地清玄
靈

SEIGEN KIKUCHI
The Psyche
INK ON PAPER
74 X 66 CM

"The soul, the psyche, the mind" is
adapted from the shell inscriptions of
the Shang dynasty of China (1100-
1200 B.C.).

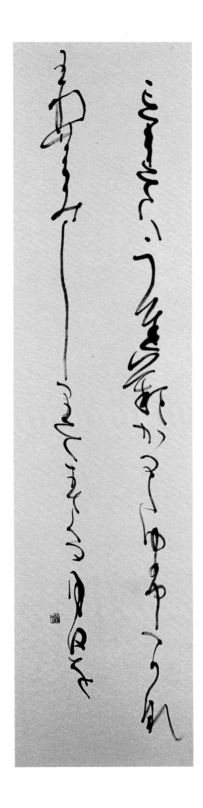

川上春泉
忘れてはうち　かるるゆふべかな

SHUNSEN KAWAKAMI
Unrequited love
INK ON PAPER
173 X 52 CM

A poem by Princess Shikishi that has
been translated as follows:

> Though he cares not for me,
> yet I have sighed at twilight
>   for years
> In unrequited love

(Translation by H.H. Honda in *The Shin
Kokinshu, 1970).*

溝呂木喜石
飛沫

KISEKI MIZOROKI
Spray
INK ON PAPER
99 X 71 CM

A fluid, gestural drawing in varying
shades of grey.

納谷古石
加餐

KOSEKI NAYA
Nourishment and Good Health
INK ON PAPER
91 X 51 CM

The calligrapher's strong and vigorous
strokes symbolize physical well-
being, and his prayer and hope for the
sufficient nourishment and good
health of fellow beings.

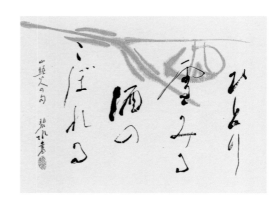

大井碧水
ひとり雪みる酒のこぼれる

HEKISUI ŌI
Watching Snow, Spilling Sake
INK ON PAPER
55 X 65 CM

The poetic phrase by Taneda Santoka
about watching the snow while
drinking sake was drawn by
combining characters and Japanese
syllabary.

勝田景泉
亀萬年

KEISEN KATSUTA
The Eternal Tortoise
INK ON PAPER
94 X 48 CM

The tortoise of "10,000 years" is
diagonally drawn in three characters
to represent the tortoise's slow,
plodding, but deliberate movement
onward and upward.

西川万里
追による

BANRI NISHIKAWA
The Search for Happiness
INK ON PAPER
93 X 60 CM

An abstraction of the character "to
pursue" rendered in shades of black
to imply the varying depths, changes
and fortunes of this pursuit.

田野倉蕚水
俳句「すみれ」

GAKUSUI TANOKURA
Violets
INK ON PAPER
87 X 85 CM

A haiku by Watanabe Suiha: "Massed
violets, emanating a delicate light."

竹澤玉鈴
並

GYOKUREI TAKEZAWA
In Step Together
INK ON PAPER
93 X 93 CM

Singing joyously, holding hands and
promenading are those in step
together.

林田翠龍
蹈舞

SUIRYŪ HAYASHIDA
Dance
INK ON PAPER
154 X 70 CM

Inscriptions on the Chinese Shang
dynasty vessels used for religious
purposes are adapted to
contemporary calligraphy.

KINDŌ HAYASHI
Facing the Truth, Staring at the Truth
INK ON PAPER
85 X 85 CM

ZUIHO KITAJIMA
A Bird's Cry
INK ON PAPER
89 X 89 CM

TAINAN SASAKI
Jar
INK ON PAPER
86 X 67 CM

REISEKI TOTORI
The Dance
INK ON PAPER
90 X 50 CM

SEISEN WATANABE
Striving Rivers
INK ON PAPER
170 X 71 CM

NANRYŪ NAGASHIMA
Above
INK ON PAPER
90 X 90 CM

SEIKAI KUNII
Prudence
INK ON PAPER
137 X 54 CM

SHŌKAKU YAMADA
Dance
INK ON PAPER
93 X 48 CM

GABOKU OGAWA
An Illusionary Skewer
INK AND GLUE ON PAPER
165 X 53 CM

KEIDŌ SHIMAMURA
Retrospective on Yoshino
INK ON PAPER
48 X 92 CM

NANRYŪ OGAWA
Accepting Poverty
INK ON PAPER
154 X 50 CM

KŌYŌ IWATA
A poem by Yu Wuling
INK ON PAPER
170 X 50 CM

TESSEN SASAKI
The Old Capital
INK ON PAPER
132 X 70 CM

KINSUI MIKAMI
Buddhist Scripture
INK ON PAPER
60 X 40 CM

KANSUI ENDŌ
The Grove Whispers and Pine Shadows
INK ON PAPER
150 X 60 CM

TESSHŌ KAWAKAMI
A Calligraphic Poem
INK ON PAPER
172 X 50 CM

KENRYŪ MIYAKE
Two Wings
INK ON PAPER
89 X 87 CM

GEKKA SASAKI
Full
INK ON PAPER
71 X 65 CM

TANKYŪ SANO
Prayer
INK ON PAPER
96 X 83 CM

TAISEN SANUKI
A Winter Morning
INK ON PAPER
145 X 51 CM

HŌRYŪ TANAKA
A Study in Black and White
INK ON PAPER
62 X 78 CM

CHECKLIST

KŌHA SAITŌ
A Poem Dedicated to World Peace
INK ON PAPER
170 X 49 CM

MICHIKO HONDA
In the beginning, there was light
INK ON PAPER
170 X 71 CM

RYŪSEN MURAKOSHI
Sūhekiran
INK ON PAPER
169 X 49 CM

KŌJŌ YAMAMOTO
Beauty Beyond Imagination
INK ON PAPER
217 X 53 CM

MASANAO IWATA
Poem by Lo Binwang
INK ON PAPER
168 X 74 CM

SEKIJŌ KANEDA
Watery Clouds
INK ON PAPER
60 X 83 CM

KANSHŪ IKUTA
To Start Anew with Restored Energy
INK ON PAPER
169 X 71 CM

SEIKEN IKEDA
A Brilliant Stone
INK ON PAPER
136 X 72 CM

GOJŌ KAZAOKA
The Truth is Nearby
INK ON PAPER
157 X 70 CM

BOKUSEN KUBOTA
Wind
INK ON PAPER
88 X 72 CM

SHŌFŪ AKIMOTO
Cherry Blossoms
INK ON PAPER
94 X 49 CM

YŪDŌ SHIBATA
A Life in the Calligraphic Arts
INK ON PAPER
156 X 50 CM

ROSETSU TANAKA
Singing
INK ON PAPER
169 X 49 CM

SUIYŌ OKAMURA
The Leaf
INK ON PAPER, GLUE AND
ALUM
94 X 48 CM

ROGAI IMAGUCHI
The Dragon in the Deep Valley
INK ON PAPER
52 X 95 CM

SEIHŌ MIYAZAWA
Living in Pollution
INK ON PAPER
54 X 66 CM

CHIKUSEN ENDŌ
Spring Winds
INK ON PAPER
156 X 54 CM

SHINDŌ AIZAWA
Mt. Fuji
INK ON PAPER
112 X 84 CM

SHASHIN IWAASA
A Message from Space!
INK ON PAPER USING
JAPANESE PAINTING COLOR
PIGMENTS
96 X 68 CM

SHIGA ONO
Dancing Cherry Blossoms
INK ON PAPER
93 X 48 CM

GENPO ASAHINA
Early winter 1992
INK, GLUE ON PAPER USING
OSTRICH FEATHERS
93 X 60 CM

KEISEN HARADA
Fireworks
GOLD INK ON PAPER
92 X 51 CM

HŌJYU KUDŌ
Circle of People
INK ON PAPER
55 X 65 CM

BOKUSUI KOBAYASHI
The Year of the Chicken
INK ON PAPER
92 X 48 CM

SEIEN SATŌ
*Virtue/Goodness is Man's
Greatest Wealth*
INK ON PAPER
52 X 94 CM

JŌKŌ MIYAMOTO
Rushing Waters and Life
INK ON PAPER
72 X 100 CM

HIROKO HIGUCHI
Mystery
INK ON PAPER
148 X 56 CM

SEIGEN KIKUCHI
The Psyche
INK ON PAPER
74 X 66 CM

SHUNSEN KAWAKAMI
Unrequited love
INK ON PAPER
173 X 52 CM

KISEKI MIZOROKI
Spray
INK ON PAPER
99 X 71 CM

KOSEKI NAYA
Nourishment and Good Health
INK ON PAPER
91 X 51 CM

KEISEN KATSUTA
The Eternal Tortoise
INK ON PAPER
94 X 48 CM

HEKISUI ŌI
Watching Snow, Spilling Sake
INK ON PAPER
55 X 65 CM

BANRI NISHIKAWA
The Search for Happiness
INK ON PAPER
93 X 60 CM

GAKUSUI TANOKURA
Violets
INK ON PAPER
87 X 85 CM

GYOKUREI TAKEZAWA
In Step Together
INK ON PAPER
93 X 93 CM

SUIRYŪ HAYASHIDA
Dance
INK ON PAPER
154 X 70 CM